THREE MEN
ON THE WAY WAY

FOR HEATHER AND PETER
THE WILLING *MOT*

THREE MEN
ON THE WAYWAY

A story of walking the West Highland Way

HAMISH BROWN

Whittles Publishing

Published by
Whittles Publishing,
Dunbeath,
Caithness, KW6 6EG,
Scotland, UK

www.whittlespublishing.com

ISBN 978-184995-087-9

Printed and bound in the UK by
Charlesworth Press, Wakefield.

Contents

Preface

This is not a guidebook to the West Highland Way but an account of three lads (Hector Macdonald, Stephen Fowler and Dave Muckersie) who walked what they nicknamed the Way Way. The book is a bit of a patchwork, for the trio seldom had time to write up their diaries and treated guidebooks somewhat casually at times, and there have been considerable improvements and even changes on the route since. Though I know it well, I've never tramped continuously along the length of the West Highland Way. I do know much of the interesting background, however, so I can supplement what they described and have added footnotes where necessary. With Hector doing a locum in Glenelg (and about to move abroad), Dave changing careers and Stephen so busy, every chance had to be taken to pin down their memories. Stephen kindly taped some stories but I had to call a halt and cobble together what I'd accumulated. They met many hundreds of people along the way but, naturally, those they recall were the more eccentric or those who were doing remarkable things with physical disabilities (and very impressive their number was).

The trio still encounter each other on club meets occasionally but have never managed another big trip together. That's life and they realise how lucky, and wise, they were to grab the chance when it came.

Sharing their experiences may have some practical benefit for those considering the idea of walking the West Highland Way – if the story does not put them off entirely – and will bring back plenty of similar memories of people and places, adventures and misadventures, for those who have put 'legs to their dream' and walked the route. After all, wilderness isn't something you define; it is something you experience, like great music.

One of the pleasures of going into the hills, for whatever activity or level of activity, is reading about similar doings. We may swot beforehand, but afterwards we read for fun. Background becomes foreground. Whether running the West Highland Way non-stop or suitcasing from hotel to hotel, there are experiences to share and memories to swop. Treasured, helpful guidebooks are put aside like dated car manuals or crutches sent back to the clinic – yet there have been no narratives telling how it was and giving the feel of the experience. You – or I – may not necessarily agree with some of the views expressed, but this is the reality, how it was, for one trio at the millennium's end. Some day I really must go and hike all the Way from Milngavie to Fort William (at a time to avoid the militant midges), for the walk sounds both suitably challenging and great fun.

Hamish Brown
Burntisland

Chapter 1

Genesis is good for you

They didn't forget themselves so much as to shake hands on the top. They did a fair bit of hugging and laughing and saying the sort of things overpaid footballers come out with after scoring a goal. Or it could have been the sort of antics like setting to your partner and swinging them round that comes in the middle of a Dashing White Sergeant. Just because they'd climbed the Ben.

Ben Nevis.

Ben Nevis, the highest litter dump in Britain:[1] 4,418 feet in old currency, 1,344 metres in dreary new payment. In case any smart-ass is thinking of writing in to say it was 4,406 feet before the ramifications of metrification, new surveying upped the height just before then, in 1964. Not many noticed. Anyone over ninety still thinks it's 4,406 feet.

The trio wouldn't have given a thought about the height. Not then. Not ever, except maybe Hector. He was sort of educated like.

When they'd stopped their celebratory antics they peered about.

'Bloody hell,' wee Davy commented.

'Is it my specs or what?' the beanpole asked.

'They're sopping, aye, but so's yir beard, an yir hair an aw.'

'So's yours.'

They were all beautifully silvered by the mist.

The mist had swallowed them on the zigzags above the Red Burn but with such a well-worn path and a thousand others straggling up and down they had hardly noticed. The summit was obvious with its big mother cairn and the scores of others (as if the bitch had whelped), the tin shelter up on the old observatory ruins, a view indicator, RIP plaques and soggy wreaths and even a dollop of old snow, dirty as a doormat.

Wee Davy took to reeling off what you might have seen, the one day in a dozen when you'd see anything, twisting his neck round as he said the names, most of which he pronounced with some originality: Creag Meaghaidh, Ben Alder, Schiehallion, Lawers, Ben More and Stobinian, Cruachan, Ben More in Mull, Rum, Skye, the Glen Shiel hills .... He made a particular mess of Sgurr nan Ceathreamhnan, added Wyvis and ended, 'An aw they Mamores and Glen Coe.'

Hector had been taken up the Ben by his father when he was about seven years old (Hector, that is, not his father) and all he could recall was seeing nothing then either. The wetness round the bottom of his trousers had turned to ice – on a midsummer's day. He muttered something to himself, then yelled at Dave to shut up.

'Let's find somewhere cosier and eat.'

'Cosier?' Specky snorted. He peered round. Ghostly figures. Disembodied voices. God, it was dank. They started off down the slope, away from the sneaky wee wind that had awaited their arrival before letting off.

They tick-tacked over the shoogly boulders, down about a hundred yards on the Glen Nevis side. There they found a hollow which at one time held the lead-lined coffin of a water tank, serving the observatory. (The lead had been 'salvaged' decades before.) They were out of sight of the summit and voices came and went like faint gasps through the strangled air, so they decided they'd gone far enough.

They hunkered down into relative shelter and took out their packed lunches. They'd come to dread packed lunches and prepared sandwiches.

'Oh no! F...ing sardines.'

'I'll swop you. I've egg all covered in mayonnaise.'

They chewed in silence.

'Well that's it then.'

'Some ending.'

'"That's the way the world ends. / Not with a bang but a Whymper."'

Wee Davy groaned. Hector said, 'Not original, Specky. And I don't suppose sitting here is either. Or doing the Way Way?'

Specky exploded. He almost made a speech. At a canter. 'Doesn't matter. *We* did it. A hundred miles, seven blisters. The whole Way. The whole Ben Nevis. And no one can ever take that away from us. Not ever.'

That shut them up.

They chewed contentedly, like cows at cud, staring into the mist, peering through into those sacred, secret memories – to them, some of the very best days of their lives. The West Highland Way.

The decision to do the West Highland Way had been made at a meet of their club at Blackrock Cottage on Rannoch Moor. The three of them had strolled along the old military road towards Ba Bridge so Specky could take a picture or two. Dave ribbed Specky that 'he wis aye takin photies as he'd no see onything itherwise'. In truth, Specky was a competent photographer and often gave slide shows or won local club competitions. In his way he was a mine of information too, as he read up about what he did. He could produce a quotation for any occasion – and did.

Heading along the brae, they met a tide of backpackers coming the other way: first, all those who had stopped overnight down near the Inveroran, then later, the Bridge of Orchy flow.

'You could set your watch by them,' Hector joked.

They seemed to exchange Hellos, Good mornings, Aye ayes with about a hundred folk before they trauchled down to Ba Bridge.

'You surely dinna need to carry aw yon wi ye?' Dave questioned after one quartet of Sassenachs had passed with burdens that would have taxed a camel.

'You'd be surprised what folk take,' Hector said. 'On one of my TGO Challenges[2] a landlady at Dalwhinnie said she'd been asked by a man to dry his soggy stockings. When she agreed she was handed *six pairs*!' After a pause he added, 'I don't even own that many.'

This led to a general discussion on just what was and was not essential and how *they'd* go about it. Hector was regarded as the authority – after all, he climbed (properly), had done over 200 Munros, been up the Matterhorn, trekked in the Atlas and walked Scotland coast-to-coast three times. Hector it was who quietly suggested that perhaps they should stop *talking* about a trip and go and do one.

'You could do worse than the West Highland Way – a splendid Long Distance Path.'

'Ah, but, we'd want you to come too.'

'Aye, or Specky will aye be stoppin fir pictures.'

'Or I'd never get Dave out the pubs.'

'I'm not so keen on these official ways. I'm not a Way Way man.' (Which was how they came to reduce the mouthful of West Highland Way to Way Way.) 'It's a pedestrian motorway. Besides, I've done chunks of it.'

'We haven't.'

'An you're the wan that's aye on aboot getting awa frae the caur.'

Hector's known locum dates decided a trip in the middle of July.

'About the worst,' he said. 'The three Ms: the Mobs, Midges and Monsoon. Perfidious Scottish summer.'

'But aw thing open.'

'He means the pubs.'

'Ah mean hostels an shops an things. Usefu services.'

'But we'd camp surely?' Hector sounded alarmed.

'Whitever you say, Boss. Hae you got a tent fir three big farts?'

'No. Specky?'

'Obviously save weight if we just had one tent. I'll try someone I know in the BB. They go camping.' He added, 'Have to be lightweight.'

'Absolutely,' said Hector.

'But strong enough for the wind.'

'Inside, or oot?'

Hector ignored this. 'I think we should be quite free to hostel or use B&Bs if the weather's really manky. Good, cheap digs when needed. We're not out to prove anything, are we?'

'Just that we're all a penny short in the pound.'

'Ah took that fir granted. Goin with youse twa. But ah agree. It should be a wheeze an no jist efter it's done. An a braw way tae roon aff the millennium.'

At Blackrock they had consumed quite a few more cans and driven most of the other BFs[3] up to bed with their single-minded topic of conversation. Little did they know the conditions under which they'd be seeing Blackrock again in less than a year. When they went out for a breath of air and to empty their bladders into the rushes the sky was awash with stars, almost milky white and strangely quivering, a touch of the Northern Lights. They shivered at the immensities.

'One could believe in God or the gods on a night like this.'

Dave let out a prolonged fart and stomped back into the cottage.

Specky speculated, 'Do you think you'll survive two weeks of him?'

'Och, he's OK. You just cut out every other word!'

They laughed.

'I really do mean it, Specky, when I say long treks, backpacking, call them what you will, are something special. There's something in it goes back to our primitive foundations. We're nomads again, exploring on, day by day, free under the stars – and yet feet firm on the ground.'

Hector Forbes Macdonald, born in South Africa, had grown up in Dollar and went to school there. The Ochils rimmed the view north from his bedroom window and, not unexpectedly, he became mad keen on the hills at an early age. He read everything he could about mountaineering and learned a hillman's skills in the old-fashioned way of trial and error. He loved going out on night wanderings over those rolling Ochil haunches, lighting himself with a Tilley lamp. (The police put a stop to that; his legs criss-crossing made the light look like a flashing SOS.) He chopped steps up a frozen Kemp's Score with the woodshed axe and hammered six-inch nails into cracks in the quarry on Gloom Hill. His parents sent him money to buy a classy Grivel ice axe and front-pointing crampons. They wanted their Edward Whymper of a son alive!

Hector's parents lived in Kenya, working on locust control, so he had lived with his gran in Station Road and then boarded. Slowly, he encouraged a few others to join his hill escapades. None of the teachers seemed to be interested. It is hardly surprising that he grew up a determined individualist, one who initiated rather than followed. In his year off before going to St Andrews University he won a Travel Prize from the school, had grants from the Royal Scottish Geographical Society and organised and led an expedition to the Atlas Mountains, partly to climb, partly to study the incidence of various eye diseases. He was now a doctor, the oldest of our trio, just doing locums while researching, plotting and planning to found something like Médecins Sans Frontières in order to return to the Atlas to establish teams to travel to remote corners doing eye operations. He'd done some of his training at the Victoria Hospital, so ended up living in a flat in Kirkcaldy, when he was not away. With his background he was a very welcome addition to the Braes o' Fife Mountaineering Club (BFMC). He'd promptly got them to have an Easter meet in his beloved Atlas Mountains. He and Stephen were good friends.

Stephen Fowler came from Southend, the one in England, not the one on the Mull of Kintyre, growing up in an identikit house off the A13 out towards Leigh-on-Sea. A gangly youth with poor eyesight, he was not one for team games but he loved running and the whole freedom of the outdoors – probably because it was in such short supply in Essex. 'There wasn't much in the way of contour lines,' he once said. He was a fanatical reader, collected O levels and A levels the way most boys collected stamps, and at eighteen went to Glasgow University – and vowed never to live among brick terraces ever again. With all his interests he joined a dozen clubs and societies, including the GUM Club (Glasgow University Mountaineering Club), but on a Saturday he would as likely be looking at paintings in Kelvingrove Art Gallery or doing a stonemason's course through the National Trust for Scotland as heading off up some Munro from the club's Clashgour hut. In his way he was a bit of a ladies' man, tall, with heavy specs, the sort of absent-minded professor figure that women longed to look after. He'd recently become engaged. He did a PhD on the chemistry of painting (so is something of an expert on art forgery) and after a spell in Edinburgh became a curator at the Kirkcaldy Museum and Art Gallery. He joined the BFMC. He was never called anything other than Specky and, if the boffin of the club, he could walk most people off their feet: the Leslie Stephen of the club.

David Muckersie was born and bred at Buckhyne (Buckhaven to outsiders). His father had been a miner but had retired with lung trouble and didn't live to see the death of mining in Scotland. Wee Davy Muckersie was not a scholar. He hated the formality of Buckhaven High School ('Lot of bloody bullshit!') and that establishment was no doubt glad to see the back of him at the earliest date possible. He loved doing things, making things and was forever down at the huts at the filled-in harbour 'helping' the old miners with their boats. An uncle in Leven was a blacksmith and when he suggested taking on Dave when he left school, everyone, but especially Dave, was delighted. He was a fast learner, which was just as well for, when he was just twenty, his uncle dropped dead at the forge one morning. Dave carried on, succeeding through sheer hard work, marrying his Betty, and soon employing several men, some a good deal older than himself. No doubt who was the boss though.

One day he received a phone call.

'Aye, Muckersie.'

'Um, er, do you do wrought iron work?'

'Aye, if ah want.'

'Oh. I wonder. I've a house in Kirkcaldy. There's a glass door at the back I'd like to protect with a wrought iron design. Could you do that?'

'Aye, could do; would you produce the design or want me tae dae it?'

'I've several ideas. Designs. Could you come? It would mean a lot to me. I want something special.'

Dave laughed. 'Dinna fash yirsel. Ah'll come.'

A few days later Specky answered the front door chimes to the blacksmith.

The ground sloped steeply at the back and a glass conservatory had been added with steps leading down from one end.

'The door strikes me as vulnerable. A professional burglar could cut his way in no bother.'

'Aye, so he wid.'

'I've sketched a few things. Ideas.' He handed the blacksmith a Rowney pad. 'Something on these lines possible?'

David Muckersie ran his eye over the pages several times.

'Aye,' he eventually said, 'There's some nice stuff there. Ony wan favourite?'

'That?'

'Would hae been ma choice. Could I tak the pad? I'll no charge you for this visit in exchange?'

'Why?'

'I could use ony, or aw, yir drawins.'

'That's rather flattering.'

'Humph. I'm no given to flatterin.'

On the way back through the house Dave couldn't help seeing the hall was full of stunning photographs, many of them of mountains and people on them.

'Yours?'

'Um, yes.'

'As I said, I'm no one for flatterin, but they look f...in fabulous – if you'll excuse ma French.'

'Anglo-Saxon actually.'

Dave eyed him. The eyes behind the lenses twinkled. They both laughed. And it was half an hour before Dave left the house. And by the time the graceful design for the door was finished Dave had accepted Specky's invitation to a slide show in the Path Tavern. A few weeks later Dave joined the BFMC and had taken to the hills, as he said, 'Like a duck tae its stuffin.' A touch of the Whillans in him.

So, at an autumn weekend meet at the Ladies Scottish Climbing Club's Blackrock Cottage, these three went for a wee walk to Ba Bridge and came back with the idea of doing the Way Way the following July. Dave and Specky, an incongruous pairing, had become good friends, with the respect of overlapping talents. (Specky fed Dave some startling design ideas which he was more than pleased to use.) Specky and Hector had much in common too (hills of course, and picking over the carcass of the past) and Dave was sharp enough to recognise, and respect, Hector's outdoors expertise, even if he'd been to a posh school. Oddly, Dave and Hector had found themselves looking at the same bowl of cacti at a flower show in Dunblane and found they were both collectors.

'So what species do you go in for?' Hector had asked.

Dave replied, 'Ah collect wans that I can pronounce the names of.'

July was *not* the best month for the Way Way but circumstances dictated their going then. Nor did the trio do much preparing. They were irregularly regular hillwalkers already and all knew bits of the area. Both work and play precluded too much thought going on the planning and Dave and Specky largely just did what Hector asked. They left caches of food at Bridge of Orchy and Kinlochleven to cover any eventualities and Hector already had Bob Aitken's guide, and they all had plenty of OS map sheets – of various ages. The route would thus not be a novel, romantic experience in the way it is to many newcomers from outside Scotland.

While the Way Way offers a real sweep of experiences, nowhere, by any definition, is there any real 'wilderness'. For much of the walk main roads are not far away and even in the wild, empty sections such as Rannoch Moor or the Lairig Mor, the marks of man are constantly around, all too often pointing to centuries of man's misuse of his world. We see a despoiled, demeaned, exploited landscape. Rannoch Moor is no longer a great forest, deer survive on the slopes in pathetic desperation, and the boggy straths are littered with sad ruins that testify to defeat. Land has to be loved, and cared for, if the marriage of man and land is to work. The Highlands offer a landscape raped and divorced.

One aspect did take them by surprise: the sheer popularity of the route and the fanatical enthusiasm of many who ticked off nothing but Long Distance Paths (LDPs), a sort of horizontal Munroitis. An average of perhaps twenty people overtook our trio every day – and they overhauled even more. This casual traffic is not recorded in their tale unless there was some socialising or unusual interest. While a surprising number passed, heads down, unsmiling, seriously struggling with their walk, there were plenty of friendly greetings and shared joys. Enjoyment is the heart of such a venture; and not just in retrospect.

Chapter 2

Footing it out

A couple, like them sitting with rucksacks in the Trans-Clyde electric train and talking of the West Highland Way, kept mentioning 'Millengavvie', which had them grinning but, after the twentieth time the mispronunciation just grated. Hector nudged Specky who, quite politely, told the couple the name was 'Mill-guy'. The name of course is the trap of traps for Sassenachs, the Scottish equivalent to Towcester. After a rearguard action Specky had to agree that plenty of simple *English* names could as easily be booby traps.

They became quite competitive, patting tricky names backwards and forwards as they journeyed on, the couple helping with some: Keswick (pronounced Kessik), Braco (Bray-Coe), Alnwick (Annik), Kilconquhar (Kin-uch-er), Derby (Darby), Strathaven (Straven), Lewes (Lewis) and so on.

Milngavie is the end of the line. The train almost seemed to be a Way Way special. Speculative excitement as packs were shouldered on the platform. There was no problem finding the West Highland Way. A hoarding-sized notice faced them at the station entrance. They dutifully turned left for the underpass.

The underpass had its walls painted with cheery murals. Specky recognised several artists' work reproduced, and a palette, leaning against the foot of the wall, almost had him bending to pick it up, a successful *trompe l'oeil* touch.

'Let's find a pub.'

'Good idea. The next won't be till the other end of Loch Lomond,' an error they were happy to correct later on.

'Food first. Chip shop.'

They returned to the bench beside the phone box facing where the Way ran down to the Allander Water. While Hector and Specky got their teeth into chicken legs, Dave sooked at black pudding, about all his teeth allowed. He even had to forgo a deep fried Mars Bar. ('Too teuchy.')

'What's she holding her hand out for?' Hector asked, looking at the draped female figure on the pedestal.

'Ach, she's seein if it's rainin.'

Specky wandered over to look.

'It's a war memorial. She's holding a flame.'

He walked round the memorial, shaking his head. 'What a waste. There's 160 names on it. For this small town.'

Resuming his seat, Specky waved his arm round the square. 'It looks just like Sevenoaks.'

Hector waved a hand along the shops. 'Greggs, McColl's, Munro, Munro, Macdonald, Clydesdale Bank. Doesn't sound like Sevenoaks to me.'

While they were finishing off their suppers a man wearing an office suit came along, briefcase in hand, the heel protectors on his shoes stuttering like distant rifle fire. He stood before the West Highland Way obelisk as if before a cenotaph. After a two-minute silence he straightened his tie (the only bright thing on his grey person), turned, and disappeared down the ramp that started the walk to Fort William. The trio looked at each other.

'He's no? ...'

'Couldn't be.'

'Right. Time for a pint.'

They got to their feet. Wee Dave 'wheeched' his rucksack round (his description later) and caught a squat, middle-aged female a good biff. She let out a squawk.

'Watch whit yir daein, ya muckle sumph!'

'Ach, awa an bile yir heid.' Dave smiled.

The apology seemed to do. The biddy went off into Greggs bakery.

When they came out of the Cross Keys they seemed to be the only walkers left in town.

'Can't put it off any longer,' Hector said. Even he, the world wanderer, felt his pulse speed up with the joy and fear that braces the beginning of any adventure. Dave had a mighty grin on his honest sonsie face.

They strode off, rather fast, as one is apt to do at the start.

'Hardly Rannoch Moor, is it?' Dave grunted.

There was a great quacking of ducks and they turned down to what looked like a wide, smooth river. There was a swan with a couple of cygnets dipping into reflections on the far bank and a score of mallard were doing as ducks do. They turned upstream.

Across the tree-edged river lay a new-mown field with a road of Victorian villas beyond.

'Still Sevenoaks,' Specky smirked.

As he said this a golden retriever plunged into the river. The owners were not pleased.

'Cum oot of there ya wee deevil! Erchie, will you look at thaat.'

'Well, maybe not Sevenoaks.'

They bore off uphill where the higher reaches of Allander Park became heathery moorland, encroached on by whispering birch and broom, that most extravagant of flowers. The sky was the colour of a blackbird's eggs and a breeze from the east tickled the first sweaty brows of the walk. Not for the first time they paused to stand, to look – and say nothing. They looked back to Glasgow's towers and out along the edge of the Kilpatrick Hills, a world created by the great lava flows of meaningless millions of years ago and much more rapidly altered by *Homo sapiens* since.

Dave had been walking ahead – which always slightly amused the other two – for Dave gave the appearance of walking with great determination, probably because he was smaller than the other two and had to take extra paces to match their striding. In reality they didn't stride and 'Glide, don't stride' was one of Hector's regular yells at club members during meets. All through the days ahead they would play tortoise and hare with less experienced walkers.

A long ride, once the Craigallian House drive, took them along through Mugdock Wood, a mix of ash, sycamore, birch, rowan, hazel and the dominant oak, very beautiful with the sun's dappling. A wagtail flitted ahead.

Where Milngavie golf course lay across the river they were confronted by a family and dog descending the brae, mother being towed by a lively yellow dog, daughter (nine perhaps) dancing round wee brother who waddled, covered in slurry-like mud from armpits to toes. At each step goo oozed out the top of his wellies and the weight of mud had half pulled his trousers down. They couldn't help laughing and, to his credit, the kid grinned back at them.

'He fell in,' the mother explained, rather needlessly.

Dave said, 'Richt noo, sonny, you must be the filthiest wee laddie in Scotland. We should pit you in the record book.'

The boy's grin expanded even more.

Dave patted the dog before they went off. He owned a Border collie cross (Whisky) which went with him on most hill trips but he – they – had decided there were too many complications, restrictions and prohibitions on the Way to take Whisky along.

Mugdock Wood and the lands round the old ruin of Mugdock Castle were given to the people of Glasgow by Sir Hugh Fraser of Allander in 1980 and are now designated as a Country Park. Anciently this was all Graham territory and Mugdock Castle the clan's principal seat. Cyclists, locals out with their dogs, other Way Way walkers were all using the woods. They just wished some of the cyclists would buy bells instead of giving them heart failure. One cyclist sped past with a boxer dog charging along behind, panting, tongue lolling.

The route wiggled across the Khyber road to continue closer to the Allander Water. Much of the ground was boggy, with vast areas of reeds and grasses and yellow flags. One stretch of path was along duckboards. Past Scroggy Hill the quiet waters of glacier-gouged Craigallian Loch appeared. There seemed to be little bird life on the loch or on the smaller Carbeth Loch soon after. They *heard* a woodpecker, a mewing buzzard and an alarmed blackbird, that was all. A corner of Carbeth Loch was golden with water lilies.

Then they came on the Green Hutters. Along the track out to Ballachalairy Yett were a whole series of wooden 'huts', many with gardens and details that pointed to proud ownership. Hector knew about this historic movement, for his uncle had had a hut in Glendevon. They were a feature of the immediate post-war desire to get out of weary city life and have some tenuous base in the country. (Older readers may recall the 'Hut Man' naturalist on *Children's Hour*.) Many hereabouts were built by folk fleeing the Clydebank blitz. Nothing shows better the social changes in a lifetime for most of these Carbeth huts now would be more truly termed chalets. A Volvo was parked by one, a speedboat by another. Parked by some tall pines was a rusty old red Mercedes van, with aerials on top and words on the side declaring 'Mobile Outdoor Broadcasting Unit'.

'Wonder who lived in that?'

'It's a while since it did any broadcasts. Looks 1960s to me.'

This 'escaping' has a long history, from Victorian naturalists to the present car-reliant Country Park users. Auchengillan camp saw generations of Boy Scouts enjoying this discovered landscape and, during the Depression days of the Thirties, Craigallian was a resort of the impoverished enthusiasts described in Alastair Borthwick's *Always a Little Further*. (There were six times as many trams out to Milngavie on a Sunday as on weekdays.) Here they would sleep rough and enjoy a social life round the Craigallian Fire, a blaze kept alive weekend by weekend.

There was a change to open landscape when they came out to the B821, which dips down east to Blanefield under the Campsies and reaches the Stockiemuir Road westwards. They walked west for about five minutes and then turned off through a stile, one which rather caught Dave's fancy, and which they would see regularly for the miles ahead: a 'squeeze' type but with the uprights held by chains so that, after you pushed through, the uprights fell back into place. 'Ingenious,' Dave muttered to himself.

They'd seen a dead pheasant on the road and at the stile a live one went racketting off. They sat for a breather. Dave told them about a pheasant encounter. He had hit one with his van.

'Near Windygates. Naebody wis aboot so intae the boot it went. Ah kent ye were meant tae hang burds sae ah strung it up in the toilet. Nae in the bathroom like, jist the wee cludgie. Next thing ah kens is Betty bawlin an when ah keeks ben there she is wi her knickers roon her ankles, cringin below the burd which was flappin awa an screamin in her lugs. Betty wisna amused. Ah'd hung it by the feet, like.'

When they stood up Specky spotted a notice, now a bit tatty, with the picture of a cat and an appeal to walkers to look out for Mémé, a missing Burmese.

'Ach, the beast will be a pair of furry mitts ba noo.'

The route onwards lay between wide walls (Tinker's Loan), always an indication of an ancient route, often for droving cattle, and led up to a wall, climbed by a stone stile. They stopped, 'gobsmacked', for there was a revelationary view sweeping down between the Campsies and the hills to the west, a world clothed with green and patched with woods. Below lay a knoll, Dumgoyach, 'like Dumgoyne wi trees on', while north lay a view of Highland hills with the porpoise fin of Ben Lomond beckoning, and hinting at tougher days ahead.

'Views like this give you itchy feet.'

The West Highland Way on to Drymen (Drimmen, not 'dry men',

please!) would all be rich farmland, a landscape sculpted by natural forces perhaps but then pleasantly garlanded by the hand of man.

The Scots pair had obviously still been thinking about place names for they suddenly produced another salvo at Specky.

'Tomintoul,' Dave said, 'pronounced Tomintowel, not tool. An Grandtully that's Grantly and Culross that's Coo-rus.'

Hector added, 'Ruthven, pronounced Riven, Camelon that's Kamlin.'

'I surrender,' Specky laughed.

With hindsight they agreed that the next half hour gave perhaps the most beautiful stretch of the whole Way Way. The route swept down past an attractive cottage, Arlehaven, to open pastures, almost bog, which were noisy with circling curlews and snipe, the braes bright with pink heath spotted orchids. Shadows swept along Dumgoyne, which might only be 427 metres (1,402 feet) but dominated their world.

'Why don't we climb it?' Hector suggested.

'What, now?'

'No. In the morning. No time now. We're being met, remember. Soon.'

They skirted west of Dumgoyach (a basalt 'neck' from which successive outbursts of lavas had poured), and crossed the Blane Water to gain a track which was once the Blane Valley railway. This dates to 1867 (joined up with the Aberfoyle line in 1882) but never really caught on as a commuter link to Glasgow. It was axed completely in 1959.

'Only another half hour. We can take a break.'

Hector slung off his rucker.

'The best thing about a rucksack is taking it off,' Specky said.

'Look at the mess!' Scattered about were crisp packets, chocolate wrappers, fag ends and beer cans and various crunched up papers – an abandoned picnic.

'I hate litter,' Specky said, 'it so diminishes the wilderness experience for others and shows how *they* have no contact with it.'

He spent a few minutes tidying up.

'I couldn't sit with that mess.'

They sprawled contentedly. The breeze had summer warmth to it. Shirts stuck to sweaty backs. A noisy lorry passed along the A81 above them. Lying quiet, they could hear the busy buzz of bees and other insects. A small rasping had Specky peering down to see a wasp scraping away at a dead stem of willowherb. Before he could comment, the insect circled off and away with another addition to its paper byke.

Hector it was who broke the lazy silence. He was watching a caterpillar working along through the grass on the verge: fat and green with front legs like little claws. He'd never seen one like it. Suddenly an ant appeared and attacked the caterpillar.

'Hey, leave off!' Hector yelled.

The others jumped.

'Whit?'

'Oh, I was talking to an ant.'

'You wis what? The man's awa.'

'No. Look! Look!'

Dave rolled over to look. The caterpillar had curled up in a protective whorl and was exuding tiny drops of golden liquid along its length. The ant was lapping away at these. Specky joined them, peering through his bottle bottoms. The ant's progress began to slow, black body staggering on uncertain legs. Eventually the ant toppled right off the caterpillar, lay on its back, feet waving feebly and then was still.

'The f…er got drunk!' Dave gasped.

Well, you should know, Specky thought to himself.

A couple of minutes later the caterpillar tentatively uncoiled and sneaked off through the grass.

'F… me.'

The ant was still lying motionless when they left.

'Dae ye think an ant can hae a hangover?'

Chapter 3

Drymen and comic hills

The raised bank along the line of the old railway contains a water pipeline which carries Loch Lomond water to the Central Belt of Scotland – as far as Livingston in West Lothian. The more famous water pipeline to Glasgow, from Loch Katrine in the Trossachs, runs along the Campsie slopes above the A81. The railway line was much more circuitous (one of its failings) for it wandered round under the Campsies by Strathblane, Lennoxtown, Milton of Campsie to Kirkintilloch before eventually deciding it really was going to Glasgow.

Dave noted 'Distillery' on the map and, shortly, they passed a signed path that led up to the A81 and the Glengoyne distillery and the sprawl of bonded warehouses. The temptation was resisted. Hector, in planning, had persuaded a friend, Andy Pollock, to collect them at Dumgoyne, give them bed and board for the night, then return them to the route next morning. 'No point missing out on some comforts when they're there.' He preached to the converted; their only iron rule was that they walked every inch between Milngavie and Fort Bill. Hardness could be modified – in moderation. Hector's frequent dictum was 'You fight every ounce of the way.'

Dumgoyne's station has gone but various walkers were sprawled on the bank, one group flexing bare feet with evident relief, and strangely ignoring a sign that said '8.5 miles to Milngavie; 8.5 seconds to a pint'. But even they hadn't time to make use of the Beech Tree Inn before Andy's grey Volvo swept up. There were brief introductions, ruckers were thrown aboard and they undulated off along the dreaded A81.

They turned off along through Lennoxtown to reach Milton of Campsie, their overnight stop – and welcome tea out on a patio overlooking a woody den, through which the abandoned Aberfoyle line once ran.

Andy was in the whisky business and enjoyed sharing his expertise in a practical fashion. Before bedtime they consumed a splendid variety of malts whose providence ranged from Orkney to Jura. His wife Val based supper round a salmon, served on a fish-shaped dish from the pottery at Lochinver. A couple of bottles of wine washed it down.

Andy showed them some slides of his West Highland Way walk, which he'd had to do over many weekends, as work allowed few days off. The benefit was that he could choose his weather. 'Not the most aesthetic way,' he admitted, 'but a practical compromise. Life's all about compromises.'

'What Andy liked', Val added, 'was having a personal attendant along. No need to carry a rucksack even.'

'That can be taken to extremes,' Hector said. 'You see companies actually running Way Way groups who have vehicle back-up and everything arranged. That to me demeans the whole idea. It's a journey of discovery but now there's a commercial element and it's all a bit contrived.'

'Och aye but, whiles, it's the stert for ithers who'd no gang tae the hills at aw.'

'Yes. But too often they remain reliant on others, never learning to do things for themselves, never making choices and decisions, never planning, just plodding along. Initiative, taking responsibility, should be a vital part of all hill games.'

No one spoke so Hector continued, 'You see it at club level. When I went out with the university club there were half a dozen who did all the planning and leading, the rest just tagged along. I'm not saying everyone should be a Chris Bonington or aiming for Everest but everyone should be trying to reach higher, improve, at whatever level. The more you put in the more you'll get out.'

Nobody felt inclined to argue. Dave, who was relatively new to the great outdoors, knew it from his professional work. While he had to do a certain amount of hack work, it was the unusual, novel challenges he relished. Specky's door had been a case in point. The fascination was that there was no possible end to the learning, the experimenting, the progression of skills. Mountains are for life.

They got talking about Alastair Borthwick's book, *Always a Little Further*: 'The most entertaining book ever written about the Scottish hills. Before the war. Madcap misdoings, sleeping in caves, the Depression days of self-help and all that, the Craigallian flame.'

Andy went over to a bookcase and took out the book. 'Like to borrow it, anyone?'

'Not just now. We're rationed to one paperback apiece.'

'What have you got?'

'Mine's *The Story of San Michele*,' Specky said. 'Hector's swotting Morocco with *Lords of the Atlas*. Gavin Maxwell. What's yours, Dave?'

'Naethin sae sophisticated. *The Shellseekers*. Ah had it as a talkin book. Wid make a great play ah'm shair, if someone wid adapt it.[4]

Books and bletherings (and the drams) kept them going till about two o'clock in the morning and even then they were reluctant to stop. But both Andy and Val had to go to work next day. They'd be met again on Loch Lomondside.

Specky appeared a bit bleary-eyed in the morning.

'You OK?' Hector asked.

'Probably. Unless my eardrums are affected. Did you hear Dave snoring?'

'No. Did he?'

'Did he?' shrieked Specky. 'Did Dave snore?'

Dave appeared, toothbrush in hand. 'Somewan talkin aboot me?'

'How on earth does Betty put up with you? I'd consider your snoring grounds for divorce.'

'Oh, she snores tae. Even mair na me.'

'Impossible!' Specky glared at Hector. 'You really didn't hear him?'

'When I sleeps, I sleeps. Sorry I didn't suffer along with you. Hadn't you noticed most of the BFs use earplugs if Dave's on a meet?'

At breakfast Val admitted she sometimes had the same problem with Andy and her remedy was to take half a sleeping pill. 'The problem is Andy always gets going before I can fall asleep.' In the end she offered to let Specky have a few. She also told of a time when Andy's mates and she were camping on a croft near Gairloch and a young dog yak-yakked hour after hour so nobody got to sleep. Pill time, she thought. But she only had a couple, not enough to go round. Then she had a brainwave: she gave the dog the sleeping pill. 'Worked perfectly.'

Leaving the house, there was a bit of a hiatus. They *all* had bought Brasher boots and though they were not all the same size quite a bit of trial and error was needed before they were sure they had their own matching left and right feet. Val went and brought a marker pen and made them put their initials on the tongues.

They sped back along under the braes of the Campsies and were dropped off at the village of Strathblane. Andy and Val headed off for Glasgow. The trio followed a pleasant track, the Pipe Road (the Loch Katrine–Glasgow water supply route), along the slope of the hill, passing above Middle Ballewan, and took to the open ground at Cantywheery. The slopes were grassy or bracken-covered and they had to cross the top of several woody streams to reach the craggy bulk of Dumgoyne. Three buzzards circled overhead and a snipe was 'drumming', a sound new to Dave. The final steep bump had crumbly crags and skirts of scree. They contoured round to the south-west ridge and up. 'A wee plook of a hill can be a sair pech,' Dave admitted.

There was a superb view to where they'd be heading: right up Loch Lomond. To the west, Duncolm, the highest of the Kilpatrick Hills, was unmistakable, another odd protuberance among the layered landscape. Specky pointed out the Queen's View car park across the valley. 'Half an hour round the hill takes you to the Whangie. Know it, Hector?'

'Yes, I've climbed there. Weird place.'

'How's it weird?' Dave asked.

'A section of the crag has pulled away leaving a narrow passage, narrow enough in places you can touch both walls at once, and the sides correspond. A bump on the left wall will fit a hollow on the right wall and so on. Makes for fun climbing. A sort of outdoor climbing wall.'

Dave had the map open. 'Richt weird names, roon here.'

'As?'

'Cochno Loch. Whit sort of language is that?'

'Ah dinna ken,' Specky teased.

'Look at them: Jaw Loch, Maiden's Paps, Tomibeg, Thief's Hill, Knockupple, Doughnot Hill, an the Whangie.'

'I like the resonant Scot's words,' Specky said, 'Saughen Braes, Auchingree, Boglairoch, Auchineden Hill …' He paused. 'Auch is a field, right?'

Hector nodded. Dave added, 'Yir no daein sae bad, Essex Man.'

'Hey, Essex doesn't do too badly either! Within a few miles of where I lived are places – mostly farms – with names like Twizzlefoot, Little Doggetts, Lower Horse, Dollyman's, Mucking Hall …'

Hector, however, reminded them they were a far cry from Fort William.

'Ah'm stiff,' Dave said as he set off, in tones both surprised and peeved.

'It takes a few days to run in.'

Cutting down to the distillery struck Dave as an excellent idea. The chimneys and pagoda roof were clear below them, the building 'clean gleaming' white through the trees.

'Can we no gang in? Ah mean, there's a free dram.'

'Quite. But we'd need an hour's tour to get one and there just isn't time.'

Specky added, pacifically, 'I'll buy you a dram at the first pub we come to Dave – then you'll have had a free dram.'

Outvoted but not altogether denied, Dave girned off across the A81, giving the fingers to a driver who'd dared to toot his car's horn at him for not looking where he was going.

They cut down by the warehouses ('Aw that whisky!') onto the route and so back to the Beech Tree Inn at Dumgoyne.

'Pub!' Dave said.

'So?' said Specky in mock innocence. 'Bit early in the day.'

'You f...er! You promised me a dram at the first pub we cam tae.'

'Oh, of course,' and Specky gave Hector a wink.

'Make it quick,' Hector said.

That wasn't difficult. Specky ran his eye along the selection and said, 'One Bell's, please.'

In the mirror he could see Dave's face.

'Pick up your jaw, Dave, and drink it down. You didn't think I'd ask for a Jura, did you?'

The next couple of miles suffer the buzz of nearby traffic on the parallel A81. There are touches of the industrial, with a small factory making furniture and conservatories, a garage, a sewage works and the Laighparks Farm Plant Centre. A thin belt of trees was being used by a parliament of rooks. Plenty of rabbits about too, and Specky, in front, saw a weasel pop out of a wall, give an insolent stare and flick out of sight again before he could point it out. He had to photograph some shaggy Highland cattle. The bridge over the Laighparks farm track had been blocked off, so there was an up and down diversion, with perhaps the last of the chain stiles that had been such a feature since Carbeth. The route then went under the B834, with Killearn a mile up eastwards and the Blane Smithy junction just along the other way. Dave scrambled up to go to the phone box at the – one time – smiddy.

'Betty's birthday. An ah'll remind her aboot Crianlarich.'

The bridge had attractive cast iron panels with decorative edges,

Specky noticed. Hector explored the map. Dave was soon back. 'Bloody phone's gone,' he snapped.

'It's on the map,' said Hector.

'Weel, the map's oot o date.'

Specky pointed out the iron features of the bridge and then they stravaiged off along the gravelly path which was being laid along this part of the Way Way. They dodged across the A81 between strings of cars and continued the well-marked line of vanished railway but the path was glutinously muddy and waterlogged – not pleasant walking. 'It will no doubt be *improved*,' Hector sighed, 'like the Pennine Way was – so the whole Way Way eventually will be surfaced like the paths of a town park.' He continued, 'I can't see any other option. You have to repair for sheer practicality. The duckboards are on the Pennine Way now – and, right now, I wish they were *here*.' The last word ended on a falsetto note as his feet went for a skite and he twisted violently to keep from sitting down in the mud. The other two chuckled.

Wild roses were prolific along the verge, the elderflowers were fading and the hawthorns had finished flowering. At a bridge they were directed up onto a small road with extensive views back to Dumgoyne and the whole rich valley of the Blane, the whaleback of moor rising on the Stockiemuir side with a swirl of clouds over it. They would, perforce, follow the minor road on to Drymen. Another overgrown branch of old railway line curved alongside awhile and they noted its pecked line on the map ended at Balloch.[5] They crossed the Endrick at Gartness, nothing more than a row of sandstone cottages, built of the warm Old Red Sandstone that runs between the volcanic world they'd been through and the Highland Line ahead. The rolling landscape from here on towards Drymen is the result of huge sand and gravel deposits from the last glaciation, a mere 12,000 years ago.

They watched the river awhile, for it has carved out pots and smoothed the river rocks till they shine like treacle toffee. Upstream there was a weir where a fisherman was casting into the still waters. ('Gie-ing his line a wash.')

'Listen,' Specky said, reading, '"It was at Gartness Castle that John Napier the mathematician[6] is said to have lived. According to tradition he was inclined to wander about the Endrick banks at night in his nightgown and cap, lost in thought. The local folk were firmly of the opinion that he was a warlock in league with the devil."'

They pulled up a brae which brought bold Dumgoyach into view, this time far behind them. Definitely getting on. But hot and sweaty, with the day muggy from the clouds keeping a lid on the world.

'But it's no rainin,' Dave mopped his receding hairline and round his ears.

Ahead, other 'bumps and bunions' stood out: Conic Hill, which was not conic at all; The Dumpling, Tom Weir's wee Duncryne; the pachydermatous Luss Hills herding west of Loch Lomond and the brown shawl of moor above the close-woven skirts of Garadhban Forest.

'An we go over Conic Hill the day?'

'Yes. But Drymen first. Early lunch. A pub, Davy lad.'

'Drymen for the dry men.'

Drymen is a compact wee place of radiating roads, a central green, with a certain calm and charm despite the callous traffic, and it had facilities – like a bank – that they'd not come across again till Kinlochleven. The Aitken guide comments, 'Like the travellers of old, the Way walker will do well to look to his purse before he crosses the Highland Line.'

Drymen is just one of several places (Crianlarich another) where the Way Way nears an obvious centre of importance for accommodation and stocking up, only to veer away from it as if any contact with beer and beds was unforgivable decadence. (The Southern Uplands Way does it all the time.) Under Hector's definition of roughing it, a call at Drymen was mandatory. On that day of sticky heat it was also uncommon sense. Far more Way Way waifs discover the horrors of dehydration than ever meet hypothermia. In 1841 the local minister grimly noted there were seven inns in Drymen – for a population of 400.

There were quite a few other Way Way men in the Clachan Inn and all seemed to have different walking ideas and overnight stops planned. There was plenty of shop talk. In several languages. Some folk even complained of the weather. Too hot.

The Clachan Inn goes back to 1734 and Rob Roy sometimes combined business and pleasure within its walls. Eric Liddell (*Chariots of Fire*) went to the local school at one time. The busy waitress distributed food and facts freely, her voice full of the warm Glasgow lilt.

'This is a scunner. Ah'm havin some chips,' Dave said. 'Wi haddock.'

'Haggis, neeps and tatties for me then,' Hector said.

'Pass the menu,' Specky sighed.

A couple, in boots and shorts, were obviously doing the Way. Their walking poles kept sliding down the wall to clatter onto the floor, which rather drew attention to them – as if they needed this – for he was a sight: plasters on cheek and chin and a white pad across his nose.

'Walking wounded?'

'Hoo dae ye think he done it? Got thumped in Glasgow?'

'Go and ask.'

'No me. No way.'

They couldn't take their eyes off the man. Eventually he gave a long-suffering sigh and said, 'Come on, dear, we must get to Lock Lomond in time.'

Manhandling rucksacks and poles proved beyond them. She played Pick a Stick with her poles passing their table and while retrieving them Dave couldn't contain his curiosity.

'Scuse me, mister, but kid ye tell us wha did aw that tae yir face?'

The man looked from Dave to Specky to Hector.

'Oh God, I'm going to have to be answering that all the way to Fort William.'

'He walked into a telegraph pole,' his wife said and with a distinct lack of feeling added, 'The goof fell asleep and walked into a telegraph pole. One with barbed wire on it.'

'He fell asleep, *walking*?'

'We came up on the overnight City Express then got a bus out to Millengavvie and set off. I was dead tired. I must have dozed off. It's not something I make a habit of. I–'

'I should hope not!' his spouse snapped. 'We wasted a day getting him patched up.'

'Six stitches.'

'Oh, come on, Dicky.'

They struggled out. She dropped her poles again. He stood on one. Not the time to say, 'Have a nice day.'

The trio didn't quite know how to react but managed to smother their laughter till the couple had gone.

'The puir bugger. Richt fusionless.'

'I wonder which hurts most, his nose, or her?'

'Women!' said Specky.

'Canny, lad! Youse is engaged, mind?'

'We can all make mistakes.'

'Aye. Dae ye ken the wan aboot the man wha said *baith* his marriages disappointed. His first wife left him. His second didnae.'

Leaving the Clachan Specky nipped over to the Spar shop for a paper. Dave wandered off and came back with bottles of Schiehallion ('Wi a name like that I couldna help it') – and a bag of something.

'So much for cutting down weight.'

They left Drymen by the wee road that runs up over Moor Park to Gartmore and Aberfoyle. They'd rejoin the route to swing through the Garadhban Forest miles. Drouthy work it proved. For once they felt summer existed. A lark sang overhead.

The tramp up to their turn-off was eased by Hector telling one of his relevant tales.

'We were up on the Red Hills in Skye on a BF meet, traversing from Glamaig over the Beinn Deargs. A typical Skye heatwave with the Cuillin like an oven. Coming off Beinn Dearg we saw a group of orange-clad youngsters. This was during the period when everything had to be orange – for safety of course – and these proved to be young soldiers on an exercise. Asked why they were wearing waterproof tops and bottoms in those conditions, we were told, "They were issued to us so we supposed we were meant to wear them." And as to why they were shoving one of their number into a sleeping bag and erecting a tent, that was the procedure they'd been taught for hypothermia. The poor casualty had been showing most of the symptoms. They'd not been told about heat exhaustion, obviously.'

'Bloody hell.'

'Worse, of course, they were not taught to *think*.'

The Forestry Commission acquired this large forest area back in 1931, so it is a well-established holding with all stages of growth and plenty of open spaces and distant views, and even some interesting birdlife with siskin, crossbill and capercaillie. Specky said some of the benefits had come from the big gale in early 1968. Big swathes had been cut through the forest. Clearing the windthrow, replanting, and better ecological understanding thus ensured the present good mix. 'You never see any wildlife under solid Sitka.'

'I can recall that gale,' Hector said. 'We were scheduled to go on a school trip to Edinburgh Zoo but every road out of Dollar was blocked that day.'

'My digs in Dowanhill had its chimney pots blown off. Six of them. They exploded like bombs on the street.'

'Ah had a wee job in a garage at the Rosie. The roof jist blew awa. Corrugated iron!'

They all contemplated a wind like that catching them in the week ahead. And observed several minutes' silence.

Down at the first wee burn they stopped to splash water on their faces.

'Ma heel's rubbin,' Dave girned.

'Blister?'

'Maybe.'

'Then stop and put a plaster on it.'

'Ach, it's no that bad.'

'But it will be if you don't.'

Dave glared at Hector. It was such a faff having to stop and take off boot and stocking and mess about with plasters. 'Ef it!' he yelled – but swung his rucker onto a bracken bank.

While Dave was plastering his heel, a couple passed, the man in a kilt. Dangling from his rucksack was a tartan doll mascot. Hector and Specky looked at each other, 'How kitsch could you get?' their unspoken comment, yet Specky had a tiny furry owl (a present from his fiancée) perched on the dashboard of his Polo and Hector never went on the hill without the long muslin *shen* that the 'blue men' of the desert wore (a present from his muleteer in the Atlas) – so who the kettle, who the pot?

A last tunnel of trees and a muscle-testing stile saw the walkers debouch onto the open moor, a pretty godforsaken place they thought, bracken to the ears and the line of the Way Way snaking far ahead.

'Thank God there's a bit of breeze now.'

A few minutes later the Burn of Mar called for a welcome break. The cheery stream was fringed with birch and rowan. A parcel of long-tailed tits worked along in erratic flight, 'jus like flyin teaspoons'.

Dave peeled off his hairy stockings, rubbed the cheesy ooze from between his toes and lay back. His nose twitching, he sniffed his fingers, and at once hurried to stand in the burn, grinning inanely as the cold gripped his shins. 'Great. Jist great!' Hector was already sitting on the bank, feet splashing like pistons while he leaned back to follow the changing patterns of cumulus above Conic Hill. Specky wasn't slow in joining them.

There was a rustle in the bracken and a hare popped out, took a look at the innocents, and loped off without much concern. A wren dodged in and out along the scrubby bank, perching now and then to let out an exuberant trill, a volume of voice out of all proportion to the small bird's size. A blip of silver droned northwards, writing a vapour trail across the blue sky. They could have lain contentedly for hours.

'Who wants one of the pub's sandwiches? I hate mayonnaise.'

'Pity we have to go down again. I much prefer the open hillsides.'

'We've still to get over the hill.'

Dave sat up and gazed at the back side of his 'Comic Hill', as he called the peaklet.

'Let's get up the wee bugger then.'

'We can traverse along the crest,' Hector said. 'More interesting than the girdle of Way Way path.' Specky had plucked some sweet gale (bog myrtle) to shove under his shoulder straps. 'It keeps off midges, I'm told.'

'There's nae midges,' Dave added.

'Yet!' the other two sighed.

Conic Hill offered several false bumps, the lumpy conglomerate rockiness demanding concentration. They undulated along. ('Like fleas tackling a hedgehog tail to nose' – Specky.)

'Lucky we've light sacks today.'

Conic Hill is only 1,175 feet (360 metres) but if ever 'small is beautiful' held true it would be on this hill. Suddenly, Loch Lomond dominated their world, a blue salver bearing strange green island cakes, a spread of water vanishing off north into the maw of greedy hills. H. V. Morton said of Loch Lomond, 'Here is one of the world's glories, and half the world seems to have visited it,' – for starters Sir Walter Scott, Robert Burns, William Wordsworth, James Hogg, Thomas Gray, Charles Dickens, George Eliot, Thomas Campbell, Thomas Carlyle, Hans Christian Andersen, Harriet Beecher Stowe, Nathaniel Hawthorne, Theodor Fontane, A. H. Clough, Gerard Manley Hopkins, Jules Verne.

The trio turned and turned to take in the panorama. To the east lay Ben Ledi and the Ochil scarp with the pencil of the Wallace Monument marking Stirling's Highland gateway. The Gargunnock and Fintry Hills extended the familiar Campsies. Through Strath Blane they could still see some buildings that marked the city of Glasgow. West of the gap lay the Kilpatricks with the wee bump of Duncolm like a toorie on its bunnet. Beyond the Inverkip Power Station lum the horizon held up the bannered hills of Arran. The Luss Hills rolled along the west side of Loch Lomond – bold, splendid hills, happily escaping the indignity of Munro altitude (just). Distantly, the Arrochar Alps nodded over to Ben Lomond.

'You'd be pushed to find a better view,' Specky judged.

'Ben Lomond's very similar,' Hector nodded north. 'Only bigger.'

Practical Dave noted the line of their hill continuing across Loch Lomond in a series of islands one behind the other. Nature doesn't often make straight lines.

'Is that yir Heilan Boondary Fault then?'

Specky was at once fascinated. He'd been on the Menteith Hills not so long before and had noted their character of lying south-west to northeast. This was simply the continuation. And it went over Ben Bowie on the other side of the loch, a hill Specky had climbed as a student, when he had been amazed at such a view from a wee hill.

'The line runs away up to Stonehaven,' Hector added.

They continued their hedgehog route over Conic Hill ('It does appear a cone from over the other side of the loch'), descending the steep southwest crest, surprised at how little marked the rock was by passing feet. Way Way walkers obviously kept to the official route with disciplined conformity. They noted a few erratics: boulders carried from miles away by glaciers and then left behind. Hector smiled, recalling a misprint in a guide which had 'errotics' instead of 'erratics'.

Not wanting Balmaha, the BFs just continued down successive bumps to reach the lochside road, the last section through trees with tripwire roots and a late cuckoo, its second syllable rusted away, reduced to '*cuck – cuck – cuck*'.

'So where do we meet Andy?'

'Right here. In half an hour. At six.'

'In that case can we go and have a paddle?'

A couple of swans were scrounging off the spaced-out groups of picnickers. The weans all seemed to have raucous Glasgow accents. Dave had learned to swim at an early age off Fife's cold Coal Coast so never lost a chance of warmer water. Specky eventually joined Dave. Hector produced a minuscule piece of soap and gave his feet a wash. One of the swans glided in quietly and pinched the soap – and very soon spat it out again. Some canoes passed, between them and Inchfad, an island which, in the mid-nineteenth century was used as 'a haven for female alcoholics'![7]

A steady trickle of Way Way walkers passed. They looked very serious, as if Dave's back flips off a rock or Specky's fighting half of Glasgow's kids over an empty coke bottle or even *Hector horizontalis* were unbearable flippancies. Dave very nearly yelled at one glum pair of elderly backpackers 'Smile, you f...ers! You're meant tae be enjoying it.'

They were rounded up by Andy's appearance.

'Come on, you lazy lot. I'm badly parked.'

They hurriedly dressed and clobbered over in unlaced boots. The Volvo did rather stick out and, with other cars lined along the road, they had to drive some way along before the big brute could turn and head off for Milton of Campsie. Andy took them back along their route, or as near as possible, and they felt Dumgoyne to Conic Hill had been quite a 'guid day's darg'.

Val prepared a beef stroganoff for supper and made sure they went to bed at a reasonable hour.

'An early start. And I'm coming with you.'

Chapter 4

Ben Lomond

Tom Weir once wrote that Loch Lomond gave some of the best lochside walking in the whole of the West Highlands. The walk fortunately keeps off the road as much as possible, for the narrow road is full of steep braes, twists and turns, and blind corners dearly beloved by the manic drivers of cars and motorbikes. The path too might win some prize for the most convoluted footpath in Britain. Redemption lies in the quality of the scenery. Loch Lomond's banks enjoy the largest area of oakwood in Scotland so the walk is mostly through that most comforting of forest worlds while at the same time, off to port, lies the magic of the big waters of the loch. Even without Scott, Wordsworth, *et al.* the area would have been accorded 'bonny, bonny banks' status. (Queen Victoria called it 'perfectly beautiful'.)

Guidebook descriptions are almost reduced to a step-by-step commentary to cover every detail. Our three soon tucked away the guide and just followed the 'amiable' ups and downs and ins and outs in serendipity mode. By its very nature such walking cannot be hurried and there were endless temptations to dawdle or paddle, which largely have to be ignored if Rowardennan, never mind Fort William, is to be reached. Any LDP calls for this element of discipline below the surface frivolities.

Andy had taken the Friday off and Val drove them all back to where they'd been collected from below Conic Hill. The four men were left to hike while Val drove on, with the promise of a picnic ready for them at Rowardennan. She might even be tempted up the Ben. Andy had been up twenty-three times. When Dave voiced wonder at this, Andy told him of an Alan Douglas who had been up the hill over a thousand times and on every day of the year.

'Munroitis,' Hector said, 'a severe case'.

Hector had been up twice. Once he had climbed the Ben from the north, on a summer weekend day, yet while he sat hoping the cloud would lift from the summit, only one person had arrived in the hour he spent on top. After he moved off round the narrow rim of the north-east corrie to the wee bump where the path bales off southwards he saw why. That minor bump was crawling with people. Obviously someone had stopped in the belief they were on top and everyone else had followed suit. 'Wrong by maybe 600 to 700 yards is quite an error. After all, the map does show a summit trig point. But Ben Lomond is a bit like Ben Nevis in that it attracts thousands who are not regular hillgoers. I'm just amazed there aren't more fiascos, except there's such a beaten track it would be hard to stray.'

At Milarrochy they were joined by a camper who chatted along with them as the path ran parallel to the road but he suddenly realised he'd left his walking pole at the campsite and headed back.

At the Cashel campsite shop they shared a big tin of pineapple (a somewhat messy performance) and had lashings of tea off an Edinburgh club who were doing the Way Way. (So much for preconceptions about mean Edinburgh folk.) There were about twenty of them, men and women, with a dozen tents and an extra big tent for dining and several wives and friends to run the catering side and move camp on in their four-by-fours. (So they didn't just use four-by-fours for shopping on Princes Street!) Dave commented it looked like a cross between a Hitler Youth Camp and a Saga Holiday outing. One Morningside-voiced male of indeterminate age and knobbly knees had a pennant fluttering overhead – from a cane tied to his rucksack. Hector smiled, 'Some of those body shapes were never made for wearing shorts. But we shouldn't be taking the piss. They gave us tea.'

Ross Point marked a change in the loch; instead of the wide sprawl of islanded water, the loch now narrowed and for the rest of the way north was seldom more than a mile wide, the buzz of west shore traffic constant and the weight of hills pressing down as if to close over the narrow gut of water entirely. At a stride Loch Lomond swops Lowland opulence for Highland asperity. Ross Wood gave an unexpected 'pech' up and over the point as if to emphasise this change of character. The last bit of path held close to the shore to avoid bushwhacking through the runaway *Rhododendron ponticum*. Suddenly they were back on the road, looking at the hotel, a piper playing, a party straggling from the Inverbeg ferry, kids squabbling about, vehicles, picnic parties. There was a view way up the loch past the pier, stout pines clung to the glacier-rounded rocks, an island offshore ('a knitted tea cosy of trees') was a crannog, a prehistoric defensive homestead. Rowardennan was a happy combination of buzz and beauty.

At Coille Mhor (*the big wood*) Dave had asked, in all innocence, if Loch Lomond was Scotland's biggest loch, and this had kept Hector and Specky arguing for the rest of the way to Rowardennan. At supper that night Specky happened to glance at the introduction of the guide and quoted, 'The way runs ... from the outskirts of Scotland's largest city to the foot of its highest mountain, along the shores of its *largest loch* and across its grandest moor.'

'See! "Largest loch".'

'Yes, but what does Aitken mean by largest; is it the longest, the biggest in area, or the biggest in volume?'

Dave yelled, 'Haud yir wheesht. You can argy the facts back in yir Kirkcaldy library.'

Specky did and, on a Monday at the Path Tavern, informed them there were three great lochs: Ness, Awe and Lomond. Their statistics work out as follows, and typically Specky drew up and made copies of the figures one lunch break at the library (which was next door to the museum).

	Loch Ness	*Loch Awe*	*Loch Lomond*
Length (km)	39	**41**	36
Greatest depth (m)	**230**	94	190
Surface area (km²)	56	39	**71**
Volume (million m³)	**7,895**	1,304	2,784

Loch Lomond is thus the largest in area only, Loch Awe is the longest, and Loch Ness holds the most water: a fair division of records, they felt. (Every day 100 million gallons of water are extracted from Loch Lomond.) The deepest loch in Britain, however, is Loch Morar, near Mallaig, at 310 metres. In all of them much lies below sea level, having been gouged out by glacier action. Specky had also copied out a passage from Tom Weir's *The Scottish Lochs* which showed the differences of the two parts of Loch Lomond rather well:

> ... if you could stop up all the streams draining into Loch Lomond it would take the river Leven two years to drain it. Speculate on what you might see if this were to happen.

Immediately below Duncryne[8] where the fields meet the shore you would make such a shallow descent to the loch floor that all the way north to Luss the islands would never be as high as Duncryne over your head.

But north of Inverbeg you would be plunging downhill in a narrow trough so deep that Tarbet would be 500 ft above you, and for the next 3 miles you would be more than 600 ft below sea-level, stumbling over the rock and rubble left by the glacier which excavated the bed.

Loch Lomond has a huge number of different fish in its waters, including the unique powan, a freshwater herring, thought to have been marooned after the last Ice Age retreated.

Val had the picnic to end all picnics waiting for them. (Later, Dave reported in awe, 'There wis *six* cool boxes!') Arrayed were cheeses known and unknown, salamis and ham, boiled eggs and every sort of colourful salad mixes, fruit and yoghourt, cake and wine, hot drinks and cold drinks. Quite the best part of the splurge was watching the justified incredulity of other Way Way walkers as they passed. They could quite happily have fed the Edinburgh mob if they'd turned up. The swans didn't do too badly.

'This is *not* the best preparation for climbing Ben Lomond,' Andy smiled. 'You're just trying to slow us down, Val. I take it you are coming.'

'Yes, this toneless perfection isn't very good for painting. I'll be happy to slow you down.'

They wisely put off starting for another hour. All but Specky sprawled on the grass. He went stalking pictures but didn't much like the flat glare either.

The path started at the Public Toilets, which called for comments about the weird ways of planners. 'Acres of woods and they plonk the loo down on the path,' were Specky's more repeatable words. The much-trodden path headed up a wide ride between Sitka spruce and larch plantings before emerging onto the open hillside. Coire Corrach on the left was topped by a mare's tail waterfall, the Sput Ban (*white fall*), on the *waterfall hill*, Tom Eas. The water tumbles and slides over 150 metres, 'like spilt milk', over schist bedding planes into the woods below.

The hillside is open grazing land and had become badly cut up by the thousands who climb the Ben every year, hence the tremendous remedial work of ditching and laying matting or rock foundations and making alternatives. The wounds are now healing well. Every step opens up the view south over the islands and the Clyde Estuary and north-west to the Arrochar Alps with the knobbly Cobbler clear. The final rise is steeper and rockier and the path zigzags up to what could be called the South-East Top.

The final crest thereafter is edged on the north-east by the cliffs of a biting corrie beyond which sprawl the forest-smothered world of the Trossachs, and a multitude of hills. Some claim the summit view to be the finest in Scotland.

'Pits Conic Hill in its place,' suggested Dave.

Ben Lomond is one of the most popular hills in Scotland and has long been so, though it is no longer regarded as the second highest, as it once was. From some of the accounts of early ascents one wonders why it was attempted. One visitor accorded it 'surprise, arising almost to terror … one side forcibly torn off, leaving a stupendous precipice'. A Cambridge graduate, William Burrell, was so overcome by vertigo on the final crest he had to descend. His friends went on 'to feast very heartily'.

Colonel Hawker, in 1813, noted that ladies making the ascent of the Ben sometimes took a piper with them in order to dance on the summit. (Shades of Boswell dancing on the top of Dun Caan.) Much of the route could be done on a pony. There were guides. A few hills like Ben Lomond, Ben Nevis, Schiehallion, Ben Vrackie, Ben Macdhui and Lochnagar were always popular, but Munro's listing of everything over 3,000 feet must have been a revelation.

Naismith, 'father of the Scottish Mountaineering Club (SMC)' and inventor of 'Naismith's Rule',[9] in 1916 walked from Glasgow to the summit of Ben Lomond and back: 62 miles in 20 hours, pauses included. He was then sixty years old. In the great freeze-up of 1895 he skated up Loch Lomond to Rowardennan.

The gang spent some time picking out interesting features, like the Wallace Monument, Edinburgh Castle, the Lomonds in Fife, the Paps of Jura and Ben Lawers, but eventually they headed down. The dazzle was going, summer as ever such a fickle season. They might have completed the circuit over Ptarmigan but Andy and Val had an evening commitment. Once back at the car they had something bubbly to drink out of one of Val's cool boxes, reorganised their gear and shouldered rucksacks which were, suddenly, decidedly heavier. Val had seen to that.

'Just some things for your supper.'

'I do so like roughing it,' Hector laughed.

Andy said, 'Well, behave then. Give my regards to the Bill and the Ben – if you survive that far. About a third never make it.'

'Hey, wha's yir frien, Hector?'

They milled about, gave Val well-merited hugs, and watched the Volvo disappear. Somehow, the day felt emptier with their parting.

'Half a mile to the hostel.'

They walked round by the edge of the loch, with its fine view up north, then followed the road along to the hostel drive. The rhodies were colourful and a couple of magnificent pines rose from the friendly oaks. A merganser went steaming along, parallel to the shingly shore, a wake of busy chicks following, and swallows swooped round the hostel as they neared their haven.

'I hope they eat midges!' Dave said.

Rowardennan youth hostel is a Victorian shooting lodge in grey granite, built to last, not over-fussy for the period and only spoilt by a crass modern extension in economy harling that could pass as a garage block.

They had a dorm to themselves, in that extension, a room with a basin and the decor in institution style ('primrose and lime') with matching curtains and token prints. The view was to a rushy bank covered in buddleia bushes and wild raspberry canes. A cloud of midges hung in the calm spot below the eaves. Not for nothing was there a notice giving a warning not to open windows because of the devils.

Looking for their room they passed the open door of another dormitory. Hector, in front, stopped so they banged into him, had a moment of chaos and then staggered on into their room with bewilderment plain.

'It was, wasn't it?'

'Aye, the mannie in the grey suit.'

'Couldn't mistake that tie.'

'See his briefcase? It was open, wi pyjamies on tap.'

'I still don't believe it.'

'Then whit wey for wid he be here?'

'You could ask him, Dave.'

'No me. He looks like somewan frae the cooncil.'

But though they saw the man later that evening, something else – someone else – cropped up to distract them and the mystery remained.

Hector was left to prepare the supper Val had provided and the others went through to the lounge with its scenic windows looking over the loch to Glen Douglas and the Luss Hills. They sat as far from the TV as possible, gazing, chatting, browsing the odd books and magazines. Specky found a battered old book by B. H. Humble, *On Scottish Hills*, mostly pictures of pre-war days, sleeping out by fires on the shores of Loch Lomond or in caves near the Cobbler. The Borthwick scene again. Suddenly Specky fell silent, read carefully and then called Dave over.

'Read that. There. "On top of Ben Lomond".'

'"Strangest were the two ... who might have strayed from Sauchiehall Street. The man wore a natty lounge suit, a bowler hat and carried a coat and a case, while his wife was complete with handbag and umbrella."'

Dave was silent awhile then took the book saying, 'I must show Hector.'

Ten minutes later he returned.

'F...in weird. An Hector kens anither. Years ago a body wis fun way up a Carngorms glen, lyin by the watta, an he wis dressed in pinstripes an aw he haed wis a brolly an a briefcase under his oxter. Naebody fun oot onythin aboot him either.'

The dining tables were next to the kitchen and Hector had set the one by the window, so they had the view.

'There's midges oot there. Teemin wie the f...ers.'

They found no difficulty in demolishing a good broth, a curry with chicken and fruits in it (plus saffron rice) and a Galia melon.

'Coffee?'

Before Hector could act on their nods, a man plonked down at their table by the window.

'Bill Payne,' he boomed.

They mumbled names in return, not at all pleased at the intrusion. Things didn't improve; the man talked. And talked. In that meow-wowing accent that comes from a lifetime of drinking Thames water.

The man was full of seeing a fox briefly near Mugdock and a squashed hedgehog near Drymen ('Dry Men' of course). Hector got a look from Dave and correctly read 'Nae wan word aboot yon caterpillar.'

The quiet Specky then made them both sit up.

'Have you seen any haggis yet?'

'Eh? 'Aggis? No. Thought that was something out of folklore, like the Loch Ness Monster or William Wallace and such like.'

'Oh no, you're just getting into prime haggis country.'

'Really?'

'Aye.'

Dave grinned, Hector grinned. Behind their hands.

'They like the woods up Loch Lomondside. Easier to hide than on the bare hillsides.'

'Really?'

Nods.

'What are they like? I mean, you eat them up here don't you?'

'Pity we didna get yon fairmer tae shoot the wan we saw efter Drymen,' (Dave emphasised the pronunciation but it was lost on Bill Payne).

'You *saw* one?'

'Aye.'

'Am I likely to? What are they like?'

'Och, wee bundles o skin. Tak a keek in a butcher's when you get tae the Fort. But, before being plucked they're sumit atween fur an feathers. An they're aye workin roon the hills because their lower legs is longer – tae tak the contours, like. They can oot-run a fox though.'

'That's their only predator,' Specky butted in, having rather resented Dave's hijacking the subject. 'You can also get them in tins.'

Hector added his mite. 'We've some tins in a food dump we left at Bridge of Orchy. If you're about we can let you have a wee dod.'

'Is it nice?' the man asked doubtfully.

'Great!' 'Aye!' 'Super!' came the responses.

'Some onywey,' Dave added. 'It's aw fixed wi inyens an oatmeal an spices an that. Some brands are affy bland. Nae guid.'

'Ours is Grant's. The best.'

'When are you at Bridge of Orchy?' Specky asked.

'Eighth.'

'Oh, we'll be staying at a hut. Along past the Inveroran Inn.'

'Oh, that's a pity. I'll be in Kinlock Leffin by then.'

'You'll jist hae tae keep yir een open then. Mind, up Loch Lomond frae here on is best. An it's no bad roon Kinloch Leven.' (He emphasised and corrected both parts of the name.)

Bill Payne did most of the talking after that but they sat solidly until he left for 'a shufty at the weather'; Dave's thermos had something in it from the Island of Jura that they were not prepared to share. When the man had gone, Hector said, 'Payne by name, pain by nature.'

'Pain in the erse.'

They sipped their Jura along with fresh coffee and Val's rich cake.

'Youse wis great, Specky. Essex Man tae the rescue.'

'*We'll* be seeing haggis the morn.' Dave chuckled as they headed for their room.

There were four beds in their room. One still remained empty.

'Thank God!'

They had only been in bed a few minutes when Dave began snoring; virtuoso vocals. Specky simply could not fall asleep. The more he tried the more he just seemed to follow every beat and cadence of Dave's performance. He'd welcome a few bars of silence and then groan as the next section came in, *fortissimo*. At one stage there was a banging on the wall and Specky learned the German for 'Be quiet' – only it was probably put a bit stronger than that. After an hour he gave up, found one of Val's Temazepam and swigged the pill down at the washbasin tap. He lay listening to Dave, same as ever – then suddenly he wasn't. Not for another six hours anyway. Hector hadn't heard a thing.

Chapter 5

Bonny banks, bloody thanks

What's the weather doing?' Specky asked from his bunk. Hector was peering out, trying to see some sky.

'Nothing much.'

'Time?'

'Seven.'

'Up?'

'May as well. Hey, Dave. Wakey wakey!'

Dave snorted and slowly came to. 'Mornin, campers.' Then he let out a blast that had Specky and Hector heading for the showers.

They met Bill Payne when they came out from their showers.

'Oh, hello Hector, hello Stephen. Feeling fit? Great to be on the trail again, what?'

They hurried breakfast.

'Let's get awa; yon plonker might want tae come wi us.'

He didn't but the midges did. They caught up on a man heading north, his arms waving frantically, while he muttered, 'I'll kill you. I'll kill you.'

'Nae point, mister,' Dave said cheerily.

'What do you mean?'

'Kill wan midge an there's a thoosan turns up fir the funeral.'

As they left the unhappy Way Way warrior behind and climbed a bit, the devils became less obnoxious.

'Wan's got me in the lug,' Dave girned.

'Knock. Knock,' said Specky, ignoring him.

'Who's there?'

'Susan.'

'Susan who?'

'Susans and susans and susans of the bloody wee beasties.'

After about a mile, limbs easing into a rhythm, they passed the drive to Ptarmigan Lodge, another old shooting lodge. The name appears on Roy's map of about 1750. The hill above is not especially noted for ptarmigan, which are at their most plentiful on more northerly or higher areas like the Cairngorms. Dave had not seen a ptarmigan.

'They turn white in winter, like mountain hares,' Specky explained.

'In summer they blend so well I once nearly stood on one which was sitting tight on its eggs. Just in time I saw the blink of its eye.'

'When they fly off they go with a whirr and glide, whirr and glide. They make a noise like frogs or someone giving a long belch.'

'Ah'm never sure when youse twa is havin me on.'

'Well, that's all gospel.'

Their forestry road began a steady ascending line, then the Way Way bifurcated and they were given an unresolved choice. The night before they'd been too engaged in eating and telling stories about haggis to have thought much about the route. They stood irresolute, with that slight lean forward of backpackers easing weight on their backs.

'"To everyman there openeth a high way and a low,
And every man decideth the way his feet will go."'

Specky added, 'That's a slight misquote. But apposite. Well?'

'High is forest track. Be easy and quick.'

'But gey dull.'

'I wasn't advocating it. I'm for the low route.'

'Specky?'

'Yes. Low for me.'

'Unanimous then. But it's like haein a committee meetin ower aw thing.'

'As well there aren't just two of us, then.'

'You can see why I've always gone alone on my TGO Challenges,' Hector laughed. 'No committee meetings. No arguments.'

The low route was demanding. Shoulders would be sore before the day's end. But at least the midges eased off their smothering presence.

'Maybe we should have carried more weight right from the start. Got used to it.'

They were still in a pleasing mix of oak, birch, rowan, hazel and the odd holly, all native trees, as are alder, ash, willow, hawthorn, yew, aspen, bird cherry and blackthorn.

'Do you know each letter of the Gaelic alphabet is named after a tree?'

'Eh?'

'A is *ailm*, elm; B is *beith*, birch; C is *call*, hazel, and so on. The alphabet also includes heather, gorse, broom, ivy and bramble.'

The going was quite rough with steep ups and downs among crags and boulders. At times the easiest line lay by the water's edge.

'You know, people who climb hills often look down on walking LDPs but LDPs are actually more demanding. Hillwalkers choose their lines, make easy choices, Way Way walkers are stuck with theirs.'

Rob Roy's Prison was the only name on the three-mile stretch from Ptarmigan Lodge to Rowchoish bothy. While Craig Rostan was certainly Clan Gregor territory, both 'prison' and 'cave' (six miles on) are perhaps spurious additions of the 'Mary Queen of Scots slept here' variety. However, it gave the lads an excuse to take off their ruckers and dip feet in the loch. They chatted about the Loch Lomond song that has the evocative 'You'll tak the high road and I'll tak the low road / And I'll be in Scotland afore ye …' and Hector was able to explain it was thought to have been written by one of the Jacobites imprisoned and condemned to death in Carlisle following the Forty-Five.

'It should be sung gently, not as a rant as so often happens. Like Burns's "Killiecrankie". Should make the skin creep. Rob Roy was also out in the 1715.'

'Played an equivocal part in the Battle of Sherrifmuir.'

Dave looked at Specky. 'Ah thocht he wis a sort o Robin Hood type.'

'They just seem to have had a talent for getting into trouble, backing the wrong sides and, in the case of Rob Roy, badly let down and cheated. He simply took revenge. He was a drover originally. And in the end died in his bed. His grave's at Balquhidder. The best book about him is by W. H. Murray.'

'The climber?' Hector asked, knowing only his classic mountaineering books.

'Yes.'

The alternative upper track twisted down to the shore to join their route, then at a bulge in the shoreline, the Way Way threaded up through a small glen (of conifers) to reach Rowchoish. If you didn't know about the bothy it could be missed, as the shelter lies buried in the conifers. The trio didn't miss the bothy: they'd planned a brew stop.

'The great advantage of being self-contained,' Hector said. 'You can stop when you like and where you like – and cater as you like.'

'We've not done badly so far.'

The bothy is tin-roofed, open at one part, so fairly primitive as bothies go. More Way Way parties used it as a day shelter than an overnight stop. A rather dishevelled figure was obviously in residence. He had an equally dishevelled dog.

'Am I glad to see someone,' he said on their arrival.

'Hi. Daein the Wey? Can ah clap yir dug?'

'Sort of. Going to Crianlarich next. Oh, Trixie's all right.'

They lapsed into the serious business of brewing. The man produced a tin mug when offered a cuppa. He highly praised Val's fruitcake, which had remained remarkably whole in Hector's rucker. They talked of this and that and, only after they had cleared up and shouldered packs again, did the man tentatively come out with, 'And which direction is Crianlarich?'

'We're going that way,' Hector said. 'Cheerie bye.'

He'd only gone fifty yards when he stopped suddenly and turned, looking baffled. Specky grinned. 'Yes, you heard correctly.'

'He didn't know which way for Crianlarich!'

The half-hour walk from Rowchoish to Cailness rises then falls through mixed woodland again – Hector noted jay, coal tit, tree creeper and yaffle (green woodpecker) – but it was mainly the views that drew comments. Through the gunbarrel gap of the Arrochar–Tarbet isthmus lay the Arrochar Alps with the unmistakable triple-peaked Cobbler clear, a view they'd noted in Andy's slide show. Long before the MacGregors raided anyone, the Vikings dragged something like forty longships over the hundred-foot Tarbet pass to go raiding the Loch Lomond islands and rich Lennox lands. This was part of a tulzie between Alexander III and King Haakon of Norway to decide who would control the western mainland and Hebrides. The Battle of Largs (1263) in the Clyde went in favour of Alexander. Haakon died in Orkney two months later. One of the odd quirks of history would see Alexander's daughter marry King Eric of Norway, and their daughter, the 'Maid of Norway', falling heir to the Scottish throne when Alexander rode his horse over a cliff and killed himself (in 1286).

The couple of miles from Cailness to Inversnaid went very pleasantly, the woods less claustrophobic but the going as dramatic, with the twisted mica schist that they'd follow for several days now adding its slippery potential. Inversnaid reminded them a bit of Rowardennan with its sudden return to a world of cars, ferry and smart hotel. They made use of the hotel's facilities and soon had a table covered in glasses, sandwiches, crisps – and surreptitious chunks of Val's cake: 'Just to tidy it up.'

Inversnaid was reached by a footbridge above the falls on the Snaid Burn, a fall which had Specky quoting the famous poem by Gerard Manley Hopkins.

'One of the more unlikely contributors to mountainy poetry,' he called the Victorian Jesuit scholar. 'And it's a real tongue-twister too.' But he romped through, with an actor's declamation, the stream churning away below their feet.

> This darksome burn, horseback brown,
> His rollrock highroad roaring down,
> In coop and in comb the fleece of his foam
> Flutes and low to the lake falls home.
>
> A windpuff-bonnet of fawn-froth
> Turns and twindles over the broth
> Of a pool so pitchblack, fell-frowning,
> It rounds and rounds Despair to drowning.
>
> Degged with dew, dappled with dew
> Are the groins of the braes that the brook treads through,
> Wiry heathpacks, flitches of fern,
> And the beadbonny ash that sits over the burn.
>
> What would the world be, once bereft
> Of wet and of wildness? Let them be left,
> O let them be left, wildness and wet;
> Long live the weeds and the wilderness yet.

'He obviously wasn't a walker,' Hector said, with feeling. 'You can have more than enough "wildness and wet". We've been incredibly lucky.' Then he grinned. 'Do you know just how wet wet can be?'

'What do you mean?'

'How wet you can become in rain, on the hill? I'll tell you.'

'Haud on.'

They let a gaggle of camera-laden Japanese tourists pass.

'Richt. On ye go.'

'As teenagers a gang of us got a soaker on the Cobbler. No Gore-Tex and all that then. We were soaked to the skin, so on reaching our tent by Loch Restil we took everything off and shoved our clothes in a bag. We weighed this once home, dried everything, weighed the clothes again and the difference was 10 pounds per person.'

'That's a gallon o water!' Dave gasped, too surprised for adjectives.

Inversnaid looks over to another gap in the hills opposite, with Ben Vane, 3,004 feet, just making the Munro team, and the bulk of Ben Vorlich, as knobbly and broken as mica schist can manage, hiding the reservoir of Loch Sloy, the pipes from which can be seen on the slope above the loch. That side of the loch was clan MacFarlane country, a clan with a reputation akin to the MacGregors. The moon was cynically called 'MacFarlane's lantern', lighting the way for many a raid.

They fell into conversation with another walker, obviously a Rohan freak, who asked if they knew the Way Way well. Would he be able to stock up with Pot Noodles at Crianlarich or Bridge of Orchy?

'Pot Noodles?' they asked.

'Yes. Now I'm on the Way I plan to have one a night for supper. Keep things simple. I've got one for Doune bothy tonight. Noodles at night, muesli for breakfast.'

'That's all?' Dave tried not to sound incredulous.

'More or less.'

'Better be more,' Hector said. 'A lot more. You need calories doing this sort of caper. Pot Noodles are lightweight concoctions with little food value for calorie-burning walkers.'

'Oh. Well ...'

The man sounded doubtful.

'There's nae shop at Bridge of Orchy.' Dave added, 'We've a food parcel left there: soup, meat and veg, pudding, coffee, Dundee cake, wine. Calories galore. F... Pot Noodles.'

Later, Specky said, 'I'd like to hear what Mr Pot Noodle says about us.'

Inversnaid itself exists as a unique break in the ranges of the loch's eastern shore, with a small road wending in from Aberfoyle by Loch Ard and Loch Arklet, perhaps a west–east drainage remnant from before glaciation gouged out the deep north–south replacement of Loch Lomond.

'The Inveruglas burn opposite might once have headed east to the Trossachs and the River Forth,' Hector said.

'A Fife river,' Dave claimed.

A scrambly section had the rock slippery from the last rain and the churning feet of those going out and back to the so-called Rob Roy's Cave. The cave (with a vandalistic painted 'CAVE' marking it) was a bit of a let-down, a mere gap among the spew of boulders. ('That it then?' was Dave's voicing of their shared disappointment.) Far more impressive was the setting, for the hillside was a steep chaos of disrupted rocks, rank vegetation and trees, fighting and fallen, through which human passage seemed impossible.

'If he ever did shelter here, he'd take a bit of winkling out.'

'Tell that to the tourists. Us! 20,000 Way Way plodders a year.'

'At least we're spared the piper and the kids selling pokes of nuts that greeted the boatload of gawkers with the Wordsworths, in 1822 I think it was. We shouldn't mock them either. This must have been like reaching Machu Picchu for us. The jungle at the world's end.'

'*Rectum mundi* of the Wey Wey?' Dave suggested.

'Hey. Who's producing the foreign phrases now?' Specky demanded.

'Och, it's jist what Buckhyne aye cawed Methil.'

Chapter 6

The hardest miles

The next hour or two will be the hardest,' Hector warned. 'The crux in climbing terms.'

He wasn't joking. The loch was now at its narrowest. Utterly wild. If it hadn't been for the constant hum of traffic heard from the tortuous A82, the setting could have been Patagonia.

' "Caledonia stern and wild"?'

'Absolutely.'

'You can often gauge the depth of a loch by imagining the flanking slopes going on down till they meet. Here it's about 500 feet.'

They stopped at a shingly strand for a paddle where a hurrying burn skittered into the loch. The oddly-named Island I Vow lay offshore. (The name is simply murdered Gaelic.)

'Must have an interesting profile too, rising out of such depths.'

'They should import a monster or twa frae Loch Ness. Stert a breedin programme. Think what that wid dae fir tourism.'

On cue something splashed in the loch. Somebody thrown a stone? The ripples had begun to spread out when something bobbed up, paddled over and hopped onto a rock where it sat, bob-bobbing, white breast clear. 'A dipper!' they all said at once. The bird dived in and out of the water several times, then flew off northwards. There was a bigger splash offshore. They just saw convulsive spray flying then a big bird rose, a fish in its talons.

'What the f…?'

'Osprey!' – which was the ornithological highlight of the trip.

A train caterpillared along the other shore, Glasgow bound.

'Reminds me of a trip when I was at the university,' Specky said. 'I'd set off to hitch to Glen Coe from Balloch but never got a lift. I could never be bothered just standing to thumb so had walked and walked. About two o'clock in the morning I'd had enough. Somewhere over there, I took a track under the railway and found an open-sided hut beside the line, so I put down my mat and sleeping bag and went out like a match. I woke thinking the end of the world had come: everything was roaring and shaking, the night in flames and reeking brimstone and fire. My heart nearly stopped. Then it was gone.'

'So?'

'A bloody steam train, probably some luxury touring special, full of sleeping punters, and it chose to empty its fire box right at the hut.'

Dave said, 'Did ye ken the original idea wis tae hae the railway built along this side o the loch?'

They lay awhile to let their feet dry.

'Mustn't waste time, today.'

'No wi ma Betty waitin,' Dave added.

'I wonder where our "Which way's Crianlarich?" lad has got to.'

'Or Mr Payne in the erse.'

'I'm surprised we don't meet more but I suppose we're all going the same way at roughly the same speed.'

Having said that, they heard voices. Walkers nearing. An unmistakable Yorkshire voice declared, 'Moi feet is killing me.'

The trio, somehow, found this hilarious.

The steepness and roughness eased off at a small shingly bay. Too soon for another stop. Somehow they hadn't taken a promised swim. And the weather was changing again. Time was stealing away the miles. There was an odd similarity to approaching Rowchoish: a miniature glen leading up to a bothy among the tame ranks of plantings (larch in this case) and Doune bothy just down the far slope, a Mountain Bothies Association shelter in one of the restored farm's outbuildings. They might have been tempted to stay but they had 'miles to go and promises to keep' so just took a look inside before moving on for the head of the loch. The eye was led northwards to the bulk of the back sides of Beinn Oss and Beinn Dubhchraig, which are really thought of as Tyndrum hills. Tyndrum! They were getting on:

> One foot in front of the other
> One foot in front of the other
> As the little dog said.

They must be about halfway on their day's walk to Crianlarich, they thought.

They followed the shore – for the last time. With a certain amount of longing they looked across to the hotel at Ardlui. A drizzle had started. It would be so easy to call up the ferry.

'Wouldn't a pint go down well?'

'Ah wis tryin no tae think aboot it.'

The wet increased enough for Hector to unearth an umbrella. Dave had not seen this trick of his and was a bit mortified. Later, he said to Specky, 'A brolly wis bad enough but did he hae tae hae wan that wis red an covered in f…in penguins?'

Specky just grinned. 'He buys them by the dozen at police lost property auctions. I toyed with the idea myself but just forgot in the rush of getting ready.'

There was a strangely shaped boulder that took Dave's fancy and he dug out his camera. Specky wandered on ahead.

'Haud yir brolly ower, please.' Hector obliged. 'Specky's gien me a lot of ideas, ye ken. He may be a walkin encyclopaedia but he sees things. Seen his glesshoose door?'

'Yes. He told me about that.'

'The devil tae dae. But if he hadna persisted ah widna be here the day.'

'Oh, you deserve each other,' Hector grinned.

Before Dave could work that out Specky yelled at them to hurry up. 'There's a big hairy caterpillar.'

When Dave 'shuggled' the heather, the caterpillar fell to the ground and curled up like a fuzzy ammonite.

The path led them above Ardleish Farm, the farm buildings in various stages of decay. They passed the Dubh Lochan, a lochan with a tonsured fringe of reeds and yellow flags.

'Say bye-bye to Loch Lomond.'

'Ben Lomond is more conic a hill than Conic Hill,' Specky said, looking through the smir of drizzle at the Munro as it rose above the wilds of Craig Rostan.

'That wis some walk. Ah'll never drive up the A82 efter this wi'oot mindin the day.'

This was another of the discovered joys of continuous trekking: there were so many good 'looking back' moments, each paying into very personal memory banks while, at the same time, there were the 'looking forward' moments, speculative, compulsive, with mysteries to be met – the right and left feet of the present which, really, is the only place we can ever be.

The Way descended the wooded 'den' (as Dave called it) to reach the flat valley floor where the River Falloch wended along a three-mile reach without a contour line. This allowed a canal to be cut linking the river right to the doorstep of the Inverarnan Hotel. Few canal reference books note this oddity, which dates to about 1850 and allowed cruising boats to reach Inverarnan. Inverarnan Hotel was originally a drovers' inn.

'We've still six and a half miles to go.'

'Should be OK.'

They crossed the bridge over the Ben Glas Burn, which, descending 1,000 feet in 1,000 yards, is really a continuous spread of falls, sadly not seen unless over on the A82. In spate it is a magnificent sight, a loose braiding of many strands. Wordsworth suggested this area should be called the Vale of Awful Sound. The farm does B&B and there are wooden 'wigwams' (bivouac huts) as well as camping space.

For an hour they followed the east bank of the River Falloch, which changes steadily in character from a douce, dark river to a pulsing, pushing flow that has carved out a seeming endless variety of gorge features, most notably the Falls of Falloch. There was no safe crossing in that hour of walking.

The glen ends with open slopes, dotted with Scots pines, and rising to the rugged Munro cluster of Beinn Chabhair, An Caisteal and Beinn a' Chroin. 'Beinn a' Chroin was the last of the Munros *and* Tops round made by the Reverend A. R. G. Burn in 1923,' Hector noted. 'The second Munroist.'

'They aw seemed tae to be reverends. Robertson. Burn.'

'They had the time,' Specky laughed.

The first golden stars of bog asphodel were appearing as they squelched down alongside the tree-choked gash of the river's course to see the Falls of Falloch, 'one great apron with an oval pool at the bottom' (Coleridge).

'Ah'm glad we dinna hae tae cross.'

'The book says you can't.'

That's not quite true. W. H. Murray in his classic *Mountaineering in Scotland* tells of how he and two friends leapt across a narrowing above the falls. On the return Murray fell in and was swept away over the falls and trapped in the pool's undertow till a chance current threw him out.

At Derrydaroch ('A bit more euphonic than the English *oakwood*') the official route crosses to pull up above the A82 on the line of the old military road (Caulfeild's, not Wade's) built over 1752–53. This passes along the top dyke of Keilator farm, so gives good views, but the BFs simply wended on up the glen, once again, following their noses rather than the set procedure.

The scenery was particularly attractive with the green skirts of the rugged hills dotted with big, dark Scots pines and the riverside bright with birch. Lousewort and the 'three friends of tormentil, milkwort and lowly bedstraw' were common. There were odd orchids too. A wagtail family was fussing about. They fell silent, just enjoying the experience of being fit and happy in the best of all worlds.

Dave, noticing a string of Highland cattle closing in from behind, pushed on to walk in front of Hector and Specky. Hector noticed the beasts and just smiled. Dave saw him and flushed. 'The f…ers have horns twenty feet wide,' he muttered. Not long afterwards a barring conifer blanket smothered the glen's slopes, so it was over to the road – over a bridge, under the railway, and along the farm road. They simply turned along the A82 for the mile and a quarter into Crianlarich, noting that the top of the road crossed a barely noticed major watershed: the Falloch draining via Loch Lomond into the Clyde on Scotland's west coast; ahead, the River Fillan eventually draining by the River Tay into the North Sea.

They had left the night's details to be worked out once they and Betty met up at Crianlarich. Betty might condescend to join them in the hostel but was more likely to find a B&B. 'I'll ferry things fir youse but I'll nae cook,' she had warned. Six o'clock in the station car park sounded like a safe meeting.

They dropped down into the beginning of the hamlet. You could hardly call Crianlarich even a village ('an urban sneeze'). The place had spread a flux of buildings along the limbs of Glens Falloch, Fillan and Dochart.

'Hey! There's a tearoom at the station,' Specky noted.

'Ah bet Betty'll be in it.'

'It's only five o'clock.'

'Well, plenty time for us then.'

They went down steps to reach a dark underpass, the walls wet stained, but halfway through more steps led up to the station.

'Bacon butty for me,' Specky said, sniffing as he entered. Swallows had chosen to nest on top of the station lamps, one immediately above the tearoom door.

'Gets warmth from the lights no doubt.'

The stationmaster was chatting at the counter and everyone said hello to each other. They took their various cholesterol supplements to a table. The cafe was long and thin, almost as if it was part of a train. The decor and furnishings were 'functional'. (Specky, trying to be diplomatic.)

'Betty will be haein tea in some B&B you can bet. Bletherin awa nae doot.'

'Well, as long as she's brought our messages ...'[10] Hector's voice trailed off. He was chief cook.

'What's she bringing?'

'Ma God, we're ony on day fower and yir fantasising aboot f...in food already.'

'No, just curious. I know Betty's quite a cook.'

'Mm. Weel, she said leek an tattie soup; a steak pie (her ain); trifle, ah think.'

'Sounds real hostel food again. I'm all for these meals on wheels.'

'Here, look at the time.'

Betty's Peugeot wasn't in the car park.

'Not quite time.'

Ten minutes later Dave snapped, 'She's late!'

'Oh, it only needs a couple of mimsers along by Loch Lubnaig and any estimate goes way out.'

There is a limited amount of entertainment to be got out of the station car park at Crianlarich. By the time Betty was half an hour late they were bored, beginning to worry and regretting the six o'clock timing which had set off Pavlovian responses. And the midges were out. If Hector and Specky refrained from comment, Dave didn't.

'Bloody woman! Ah'm stairvin!'

He paced the car park like a POW restrained by barbed wire.

'Ah'll gang an check the cafe.'

'It may be shut.'

'Watch ma bag.'

He clanged into the underpass and as he did so a figure entered from the other side. They almost collided at the stairs. There was a dual, simultaneous exclamation, roughly translated as, 'Where the hell hae ye been?' as diminutive Dave and Betty ('built like a combination of Ben Nevis and the Paps of Jura' – Specky) confronted each other.

'I wis at the hostel tae gie ye a richt piece o ma mind. Could you no be bothered waitin in the car park?'

'We've been stanin in the f...in car park since before five!'

'You have not!'

'We have f...in so. The others are there the noo.'

'Where?'

'*There*, ya gowk,' and Dave pointed whence he'd come.

'Well, I've been *there*.' Betty pointed whence she'd come. 'In the car park.'

'Car park?'

'Aye, that wis the idea.'

'But we're in the car park, *there*.'

More or less simultaneously they both said, 'Oh no! There's two f...in car parks!'

Betty had left her car at the hostel. Dave was given an ecstatic welcome from Whisky. They offloaded the goodies Betty had brought, made arrangements for Tyndrum and watched her drive off for her B&B. The youth hostel lay over a burn, edged by shrub roses, rowans with berries already forming, flowers up the drive and hanging baskets over the porch door. The building sprawled among the trees like an opulent bungalow. They were given a friendly welcome at reception, noted the bustle of supper preparations by the many Way Way walkers and were soon involved themselves. Damp socks were hung up in the drying room.

The walls were covered with various maps and large prints of the hills, and a group of photos showed the old wooden shack on stilts that this building had replaced. On semi-open-plan style, it had an uncluttered dining room, vases of flowers on the windowsills, arty lighting arrangements – and the television was not switched on! They liked their home for the night.

'An nae Bill Payne.'

They told the warden about him.

'You'll find all types,' she smiled. 'Look.'

Three girls, quite unlike outdoor types, were dragging a big wheeled case that had broken its handle. The spectators were so mesmerised by the sight that no one went to their aid, besides which they were going into the women's quarters. As the girls went puffing and clattering out of sight, one of them said, 'Bags first go with the hairdryer.'

The warden sighed. 'God knows what they think they're doing. They have their bags taken door to door and they walk quite inadequately turned out. Each bag has to be paid for so they cram everything into one big case to save money and then can hardly move it. And they call it backpacking!'

'She did say "hairdryer"?'

'Oh aye, that's nothing. You wait till you see them later. Painted toenails will be the least of it.'

After a pause the warden continued, 'You may catch up a remarkable couple in the next few days. In their eighties. He was struck down by some wasting ailment and now can hardly bend and has a shrivelled leg – and she's diabetic. They had small packs but still looked tired on arrival here. But they said they'd take a day off and bag a Munro. They had to get to the post office anyway as their daughter had sent on parcels of everything they needed and they'd send back their change of clothes, used maps and so on. When they walked in, I asked, 'Walked far?', thinking Rowardennan quite a step for the look of them, but she smiled and said, "Just from Leeds."'

'Walked from Leeds? Or belonging to Leeds?'

'Walking. And aiming for Inverness. Next year Inverness to John o' Groats.' After a pause the warden continued, 'When told he would never walk again the man apparently said, "Sod that!" Used to walk to a pub every day and would increase the distance regularly. He could only be comfy on bar stools of a certain height so had this height marked on the stick he carried. If a pub's stools didn't measure up he'd go on to the next pub. Said this was his real therapy. Then they started at Land's End two years ago. Ended at home last year. Said he was beginning to feel a bit old so really pushing on this year.'

'Good excuse tae gang ben aw they pubs,' Dave said. 'Ah'll buy him onythin he likes. F…in marvellous.'

Chapter 7

Westering ho

Our trio, not being regular LDP baggers but ordinary mountaineering club members, tended to treat all guidebooks with a certain casualness. Theirs was the cry 'This is my own, my native land!' (in Specky's case by adoption) and they followed the ancient right to stravaig as they would. Directions were more suggestions than imperatives. The last two days' walking, after all, could have been reduced to one instructional sentence: 'Keep Loch Lomond on your left.' They read the guidebook largely because they were fascinated with all they saw and wanted to know about the background. 'Why?' more than 'What?'

This somewhat casual attitude had them setting off good and early but not wisely. They strode off westwards out of Crianlarich, dodging a lorry at the railway bridge, still half asleep and cholesterol choked, Dave having produced, thanks to Betty, a fry-up of frightening size and variety. Judging by the marked verge, they were not the first to simply follow the A82 – which was to prove the most dangerous hour they were to have on the Way Way. Car drivers seemed to be blind to their presence. Then they had a piece of luck. Dave found a length of white plastic guttering (which looked like metal) and he proceeded to swing this with some vigour as he stomped ahead. At once there was a change in behaviour from the speeding car drivers. They swung out violently to pass the group. One driver even turned to shake a fist at them.

'The f...ers!' Dave laughed. 'They'd shave us wi'oot a thocht, but risk their paintwork, naw, naw.'

Specky and Dave then became engrossed in conversing about railway interests, so they sailed past the small opening with a post bearing the Way Way logo. Hector had broken stride to look at a pink ragged robin, so he did see it and called the other two back.

'F…in bloody road!'

'Moi feet is killing me,' Specky added.

He wasn't exaggerating. When they'd taken the footpath across a rushy field end to a kissing gate by the bridge over the River Fillan Specky had to stop and plaster a hot spot on one heel and a blister on the other.

'Sorry to hold you up.'

'Had to stop onywey. That fourth cup of tea wis a mistake.'

Specky disappeared (a photo call): pink and white foxgloves by the river, the classic view back to the triptych of Ben More, Stobinian and Cruach Ardrain. He caught them up at the old Kirkton graveyard, the site of St Fillan's chapel.

St Fillan is associated with several places in Perthshire, though, oddly not the St Fillans on Loch Earn – named after an earlier leper saint. His name was known to the trio because of his cave-church at Pittenweem, in Fife. He became abbot of a monastery on the Holy Loch but resigned to live in the Highlands as a hermit, here in Breadalbane. One legend has him taming a wolf through his prayers.

Two relics of St Fillan are housed in the National Museum of Scotland in Edinburgh: a bell and the head of a crozier. The head of St Fillan's crozier (called the Quigrich, which sounds like something out of Harry Potter) had gone to Canada in 1818 but was recovered in 1877 by the Society of Antiquaries of Scotland, the precursors of the museum in Chambers Street. A beautiful piece of intricate silverwork, it dates to the fourteenth century but contained an older head within its casing. The Quigrich is rightly regarded as one of Scotland's most treasured antiquities. Specky and Dave made a point of seeing the relics several weeks later, once the Edinburgh Festival was over. Dave, in particular, was entranced and began something which may well change his life. While working in iron during the day his evenings have been spent learning how to work in silver. Night classes and City and Guilds courses keep him busy most nights, to Betty's joy and the Buck and Hind's loss, though Monday nights in the Path Tavern with the BFs is still sacred. Specky recently forecast to Hector that in a couple of years Dave would sell out the Leven smithy and be making his living as a silversmith.

'All because we went off on the Way Way!'

They followed a farm track onwards to another sprawl of farm buildings at Auchtertyre. Sheep were milling about in a big shed. Walkers were welcome, with an unusual array of wooden camping wigwams and chalets. There was a shop, so they stopped to down a pint of milk each while they chatted. There was no problem about going up the Munro Ben Challum (*Malcolm's Hill*). A path signposted for 'Woodland Walk' went up the east side of the Allt Gleann a' Chlachain.

There were a dozen more wigwams and chalets, which they passed before dipping into the wood. A right fork joined the farm track, which ran under the viaduct of the railway line. They were just coming out from below the viaduct when a train (alumina trucks) went thundering over – giving an enthusiastic hoot that came near to stopping hearts.

The early promise had gone. A roller blind of cloud was being inched down. Dave said it was because of Specky taking photos.

They hid their rucksacks among the birches.

'It's like floating wi'oot that weicht. Nae wonner folks get theirs taken on every day.'

The green fur coat of bracken clawed at their legs and they angled up soon rather than later. Too late they noted a farm track up the other side of the glen, a glen full of the tracings of old shielings, as its name suggested. At about the 600-metre level they were into cloud, a steam-like summer vapour. For safety Hector traversed north to hit the Allt Coire nan Each, and then they followed up the streamside.

'Are ye no takin a bearin wi the compass?'

'No need. It's a defined-enough summit so if we just go uphill leftwards a bit we must land on the cairn.'

Specky added, 'It's easier zigzagging anyway. Walking on a bearing can be a bind.' He laughed. 'Remember that time on the Drumochter Four, Hector? You took a bearing on a bump and then it got up and walked away. It was a sheep.'

'Well, what about you, Specky, up in Sutherland? We were caught in the dark, Dave, and the ground was all lochans and bare bumps so Specky was being ultra careful. Counting steps even.'

'A hundred and seven, a hundred and eight, a hundred and nine,' Specky intoned.

'A hundred and ten, splash, splash, splash,' Hector concluded. 'Up to his waist! And it was November.'

Ben Challum is 1,025 metres (3,363 feet), so a 'considerable protuberance' in Doctor Johnson's description of a Glen Shiel hill. The summit area was a dome rather than a well-defined peak and the mist had a glow to it which, while indicating thin cloud overhead, made for an uncomfortable glare. Hector strode on, however, and suddenly they were at the big cairn. (No trig, which is strange, the hill being the highest in that part of Strath Fillan.)

'"Well, we knocked the bastard off",' Hector shouted, quite relieved.

The others looked startled. That was strong language, coming from Hector.

'That's a quotation,' he grinned.

'Oh, aye.'

'It's what Hillary said when he came down from the top of Everest.'

'It wasn't in the Everest book.'

'Weel, it widna be, wid it?'

'Pity about the view – or lack of it. Glen Lochay must lie down that way. Challum looks its best from there. And north-west of us is the only close grouping of Corbetts where you can do five in a day. You don't get a Cluanie Ridge or a Mamores line-up with Corbetts.'

'Och, they're jist auld men's Munros,' Dave teased.

'You may change your mind when you're an old man then, Dave. If you're wise you'll do them whenever possible. Too many just tick Munros and do nothing else. What's the hurry? You know, last year I met a kid at Braemar youth hostel who said he was a Munro bagger. When I asked him how many he'd done, he said "Five".'

Specky interrupted. 'I'm getting cold. Are we going to eat?'

'Let's get down lower first. We don't *have to* eat at the summit always.'

They headed south over another minor summit. The rain started. Dave described their descent as 'walking in white air'. Once below the cloud they hurried on. Dave then lagged behind muttering away.

'Bit thundery back there.'

They waited. The mutterings grew louder. 'Had the whole f...in world tae flee in an chooses tae land in ma e'en.'

'Stop rubbing it.'

'It f...in stings.'

'Look up ... now hold still ... There!' Hector held out the corner of his travel-worn hanky to show Dave the offending speck. A midge no doubt.

'Is that aw?'

The rain seemed to be taking time out, so they paused for a bite to eat before returning to their rucksacks above Auchtertyre. Hector had warned them of the danger of hiding rucksacks so well that they couldn't find them again.

The track from Auchtertyre went along under a steep, grassy bank full of flowers – a ridge of fluvial-glacial material in geology-speak. 'Near the A82 is the Holy Pool,' Specky informed them, book in hand.

'Holy Pool?'

'In the good old days lunatics were stripped and dumped in the river, then bound hand and foot before being left overnight in the graveyard with just a covering of straw and St Fillan's bell on their heads. Supposed to cure them.' Hector added, 'An 1843 guidebook commented that this was "a degrading superstitious rite *to this day*"– 1843!

After crossing the busy road the bridge on the Cononish glen track brought them to known ground, as Hector and Specky had done Ben Lui as their 'Boots Across Scotland' peak. (Boots was a charity's attempt to have someone atop all the Munros at the same hour on the same day – which failed by a handful, thanks to a fairly vicious distribution of weather.) They came on a little lochan which Specky said could be the site of the skirmish in 1306 when Robert the Bruce was defeated by the Comyn supporters, the Macdougalls of Lorne.

'He'd just been crowned at Scone, in March, been beaten by an English force at Methven (west of Perth) in June and fled west, only to come to grief again here. Not a good year on the whole.'

Bruce was ambushed by three Macdougalls. The king, remarkably, killed all three of his attackers but his plaid and its fastening brooch had been torn off – and became a Lorne treasure till lost in a fire.

Dalrigh (pronounced Dal ree) is a strange place of bumps and hollows, created by the dumper trucks of glaciation, surrounded by bold hills and stabbing glens. Some attractive old Scots pine woodland girdled Beinn Dubhchraig's lower slopes, while graceful Ben Lui and scalloped Beinn Chuirn lay up the Cononish; but thereafter they came on several less attractive features: Tyndrum itself, the massed conifer plantations on all sides, and the scars of lead mining which so poisoned the ground that even after two centuries nature hasn't healed the wounds. Tyndrum is pronounced Tine-drum (not tindrum), an illogical contrast to Drymen, which is pronounced Drimmin. The name comes from *tigh-druim*, house of the ridge, and in olden days people thought the hamlet must be one of the highest in the country. It is the smallest town (well, place) in Britain that has *two* railway stations.

The trio crossed a footbridge into the Pine Trees campsite. They called in at reception to check Betty had left their supplies and tent (Dave had an ice cream), then went up to the main road and along to see what Tyndrum had to offer. They wanted a Harvey map of Ben Nevis and the large tourist office would have that. The sheer incongruity of finding a Little Chef next door drew them in after buying the map.

'A pot of tea for six,' Hector ordered.

'With toasted teacakes,' Specky added.

They picked out one or two groups of obvious fellow Way Way folk. One lot seemed to be German. They smiled when they overheard one female tell another, 'It's our fifth day and we're still speaking to each other.' Someone else said, 'Oh, my feet do ache.'

Conversation drifted on to the oddity of Tyndrum having two stations.

'So had Crianlarich.'

'It had twa lines, kept separate ba politics, nae geography.'

'How?'

Specky explained, 'The Callander–Oban line opened its station at Crianlarich first, then the West Highland line, Glasgow to Fort William, opened later. There was a spur to link the lines and one station would have done but they preferred to ignore each other. There's no Callander route now, thanks to a landslide in Glen Ogle, so both Oban and Fort William come from Glasgow. So Strath Fillan has a railway on each side and Tyndrum two stations. Our campsite is on the old goods yard of the Lower Station.'

Tyndrum's always been a crossroads sort of place, very big back in the droving years. The intrepid traveller Mrs Sarah Murray stayed at the inn in 1799 and it was crammed with drovers: 'a perfect uproar: my servants could not get a place to put their heads in. My man took his sleep in the carriage: and the poor horses were almost crushed to death in the stables.'

Queen Victoria passed through in 1873 and noted in her diary of 22 September : 'We reached Tyndrum, a wild, picturesque and desolate place in a sort of wild glen with green hills rising around.'

Specky and Dave could have gone on talking railways all night.

Quite a few other walkers passed (heading west) and Hector commented that many were dressed in black or navy blue. He'd assumed most walkers knew that midges preferred dark clothing. Thank goodness they'd not been camping on the occasions, so far, when the devils were about. A couple passed, heavily laden, poles clicking, dressed in matching black T-shirts and shorts. Hector shivered involuntarily. Midge trophies.

One man passing set them giggling. 'Must have gone mad in Tiso's,' Specky suggested. He wore the latest designer clothing (trousers that unzipped to become shorts) and a rucksack which seemed to truss him like a Christmas turkey. A tube led from the rucksack so he could drink without pausing. Round his neck or on a belt were camera, bum bag, a GPS pouch, mini karabiners and map case. He had huge boots on his feet, a baseball cap on his head, two walking poles and was talking into his mobile phone, while earphones indicated a cassette player in his multi-pocketed shirt. There was no sun but he wore purple shades – and earrings.

'F…in walkin catalogue.'

'Hey, look who's passin now.'

A couple were walking, on and off the verge, the woman in front, Boadicea-like, cars swerving as they neared, the man behind, limping. There was a big white patch on the man's nose.

'Well, they got this far,' Hector said.

'But why are they walking eastwards? Not camping, surely.'

'An whit's he done noo tae be limpin?'

They spent an amusing ten minutes creating scenarios to answer their own questions. Suggestions became somewhat ribald and their laughter was receiving glares from their 'chips with everything' neighbours.

'Let's gang, afore they chuck us oot.'

Refreshed with their tea for six and toasted teacakes, they made their way to the campsite where they retrieved all the gear and the tent. 'Travel-lite pickup point,' said a notice.

They found a spot as close to the river as possible. The tent was pulled from its bag – and would never go back into it. One of the more stupid of regular sales gimmicks is making tent packages as small as possible: fine in the factory but just try getting a wet or frozen tent back in its original bag! They never did.

'Have you put it up before?' Hector asked.

Specky looked embarrassed.

'Well, no, actually. I meant to. But it's all there and good as new. I was assured of that, or I would have.'

'Most tents are fairly obvious. Let's see.'

Hector turned the material over several times while Specky and Dave opened out the poles.

'Whit a length!'

'They make hoops.'

'Right, there's the sleeves. Push the poles through. Don't pull them Dave, or they come apart.'

Dave promptly did what he shouldn't. 'What a fiky system,' he thought as he tried to work the poles together again through the slithery sleeve material. Eventually the dome was up and they waltzed around to site the door facing away from the lightest of westerly breezes; the wind could always blow up again.

'If we don't bother with the inner we'll have more headroom,' Hector commented. 'I don't think it'll rain. Want to chance it?'

'Sure.' 'Aye.'

Hector spread the inner, kicked off his boots and took in their gear as they unpacked. Hector, as chief cook, went in the middle. Hector said he was happy to cook – 'in self-defence'.

One of the facts of camping is that gear in a tent takes up a hundred times the space of gear in a rucksack. When the other two crawled in there was a marked element of slumming it. Three men in a tent is a good test of friendship.

They hadn't been rummaging very long before starting to scratch. Midges again. Well, July was open season on humans.

'Oh, no!'

'We'll have to put up the inner. The front is mosquito netting, thank heavens.'

This was easier said than done. They and their belongings were lying on top of the inner. They tried to stack everything at the door but, apart from the gear, there were their three bulky bodies sweating, swearing and struggling in the restricted space. They had to open the door, eject the shambles of gear, and while Specky and Dave pranced about like performing Lippizaners, Hector struggled with getting the inner attached to the outer. 'Should have practised at home,' he muttered.

'F...in hurry up! Ah'm itchy aw ower.'

They threw everything in any old how, scrabbled in themselves, closed the parabola of zip and lay back. There were still midges in the tent. A fuss of them gathered at the top of the dome, from whence periodic dive-bombing attacks were made on the civilian population. Suddenly Dave, in unusually quiet tones (of shock?) muttered, 'Ah dinna believe it. Ah dinna believe it. Look!'

They looked. The front of the inner was mosquito netting, 'allowing free movement of air while affording protection against insect pests' (according to the instruction manual) but the swarms of midges must have been illiterate for they were simply crawling through. They watched, mesmerised. The inside of the netting began to fur over with midges, then one by one the specks flew on in search of the blood they craved.

'F... me!' Dave breathed.

Hector desperately rummaged among the mass of gear till he came up with a box garishly labelled Moon Tiger. He fiddled with a stand then balanced a green coil on it, took another five minutes to find a lighter, lit the coil and placed the contraption near the door. A deadly wisp of smoke curled upwards and they watched gleefully as midges began to detach from the netting and fall onto the groundsheet.

Half an hour later the tent was full of the stinking smoke.

'If it kills midges, what's it doing to us?'

Hector read the packet: 'Do not use in confined spaces.'

'So, we get poisoned or bitten tae deeth.'

'Are there no remedies for midges?' Specky groaned.

'Och aye,' Dave said. 'Emigration. Hae you no heard o the Highland Clearances?'

Chapter 8

The pass with no name

Specky woke slowly and turned over. There was a strange purring sound in his ear. Not Dave snoring, for that gentleman was in snuffle-and-snort mode right then. He could almost *feel* the noise. Weird. Worrying. Was he going nuts? He opened a sleepy eye. Snug by his shoulder was a grey kitten. At Specky's registering the fact of its existence, the creature went into overdrive, then uncurled to poke a cold nose into Specky's eye.

'OK. OK,' he said, 'So, I'm awake. And good morning to you too.'

Dave choked on a snort and said, 'Eh?'

'Nothing. It's only six o'clock.'

'Wassanoisethen?'

'Go back to sleep.'

A minute later Dave was snoring. Specky sighed and wiggled out of his sleeping bag. 'Sorry, puss, you'll have to move.'

He dressed and set off for a stroll.

'Coming then, you Gumbie Cat?'

Specky then looked round quickly. Nobody else was about, luckily. You don't take a cat for walkies.

This one went walkies, though, once Specky had tucked his laces out of sight. He'd nearly stood on the kitten.

There were seventeen tents which could have been those of Way Way walkers. From four of them came snores (three bass, one baritone). Only two tents were of the same make. At an old-fashioned orange Vango a pair of boots had been left sticking out so all the rain off the flysheet had been going into them. There were a lot of dirty dishes lying about. The kitten stopped to inspect one or two, would shake a head or sneeze and gallop after Specky, tail held up in the air. The kitten didn't seem to mind the wet grass and its underneath became saturated. Specky presumed any cat living in Tyndrum would have acclimatised to wet. At a wide puddle, though, the kitten remained behind and miaowed pitifully. Specky came back and picked it up. The creature scrambled onto his shoulder, draped round his neck and settled happily, purring away. Growl Tiger. Specky wondered what was the world record for the longest known cat purr. And could the purr be heard from the next cubicle in the Gents? He returned to the tent and roused the other two.

The trio were walking towards the main road to start the day's effort when they noticed a dog heading towards the shower block. What made this unusual, though, was that the dog was towing a tent in its wake. The dog was big, the tent was small and tying the beast to the tent pole while master went to shower had been a mistake. The contents were spilling, piece by piece, so it was possible to trace it back to where the unknown innocent had pitched. Two toddlers were dancing along, enjoying the game and keeping the animal company, while one or two adults stood at the door of the shower block, as shocked as receptionists at the Ritz faced with a delegation of nudists. The trio passed by on the other side. You need a real reason to take off a rucksack immediately after you've struggled into it.

As they walked on, Specky suddenly noticed Dave had tied a small teddy bear on top of his rucksack. He nudged Hector and nodded. Dave must have felt their silent amusement, turned, caught them grinning, and glared.

'Betty gied it tae me at Crianlarich. Ah forgot.'

'Could you not keep forgetting?'

'Shit. She's bound tae ask.'

Dave bought a paper from the Clifton store to check on the football results. Neither Raith Rovers nor East Fife received any commendation. They bought a few day nibbles and some cans of ale.

'Got to survive as far as Bridge of Orchy.'

'Let's move then. The midges are out.'

Their steady uphill tramp was along the line of Caulfeild's military road, which they would (or could) keep to nearly all the way to Fort William, relatively easy walking, however grand the surroundings.

Near the top of the pass they skirted the big blue tanks of Tyndrum's water supply, less intrusive now as a scrub of trees surrounds the site. There was a last glimpse back to the tat that is Tyndrum.

Afoot or awheel, one of the most memorable of Highland views explodes into sight on the pass. Specky went into photography mode and cursed when his camera ran out of film and he had to change films. The midges welcomed him. Specky later found that maps and guides, however old, don't seem to have a name for this pass of passes, which is on the Scottish watershed, is the Perthshire–Argyll boundary, has road, rail and Way Way through it, and was a drovers' route and military road in the past. Can any reader help? It must have had a name.

Beinn Odhar (pronounced Or) flanking on the east rises in one of the steepest continuous slopes in Scotland. Over the pass all the drainage runs to the River Orchy (and on to Loch Awe and the sea) so the north–south watershed goes into spasms as it wiggles through the convoluted complexities. Hector tried to trace the line on the map and gave up. 'If you want to read all about the watershed, get a copy of Dave Hewitt's book, *The Watershed Walk*. Fascinating. He actually followed it.'

Dave only had eyes for the hill ahead. 'Now, that is whit ah'd caw a conic hill.'

'Beinn Dorain,' Hector named the peak of peaks, 'the hill forever associated with Duncan Bàn MacIntyre, one of the great Gaelic poets. He wrote "Farewell to the Bens" after his last ascent, when he was seventy-eight.'

MacIntyre was born poor and served much of his time as gamekeeper or forester; in Glen Etive he wooed and won the bailiff's beautiful daughter. He was to retire ultimately from the Edinburgh City Guard. He was one of the earliest to *express* feelings for the mountains.[11] He toured to help sell his books, and was noticed in Fort William singing from a volume held upside down. (He was illiterate!) He died aged eighty-eight in 1812 and is buried in Greyfriars Churchyard in Edinburgh, but his real monument is this landscape: the soft waters of Loch Tulla, the red-barked pines and the snub-nosed cone of Beinn Dorain.

The Way Way does a gentle traverse across the skirt of Beinn Odhar then dips to go under the railway, by one of the 200 'creeps' on the line, and joins a good track onwards for the Auch glen. The railway meanwhile makes a huge horseshoe curve to save on gradients (and construction costs). Coming round a bend, the view explosively dominated by the sweeping lines of Beinn Dorain, they came on a sight that brought them to an instant stop. On the track stood a table, covered in gently waving cloth and laden with a cake and all manner of goodies, a bottle of

All smart and tidy: the start of the walk in Milngavie.

In Mugdock Wood.

The Strathblane style of stile.

A notice by the Beech Tree Inn.

Dumgoyne above Strathblane.

The Clachan Inn, Drymen.

*From Conic Hill to the islands in Loch Lomond marking the
Highland Boundary Fault.*

Rowardennan youth hostel, welcome haven on Loch Lomond's shore.

Bracket fungi in the fine Loch Lomond woodlands.

The Inversnaid Falls that inspired Gerard Manley Hopkins.

Looking to the summit of Ben Lomond.

The bonnie, bonnie banks of Loch Lomond.

*A stag in summer 'velvet'
(covering the antlers).*

Below: *Cruach Ardrain
above Crianlarich.*

*Alternative
accommodation
at Auchtertyre.*

To Beinn Laoigh from Auchtertyre.

The classic view to Beinn Dorain from the pass above Tyndrum.

Refreshments at the Bridge of Orchy Hotel.

Stepping out – over the historic Bridge of Orchy.

Reporting home?

Heading up the Mam Carraigh from Bridge of Orchy.

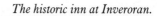

A warning in the ancient pine forest of Doire Darach by Loch Tulla.

The historic inn at Inveroran.

The monument marking the birthplace of poet Duncan Bàn MacIntyre.

Ba Bridge in the heart of Rannoch Moor.

Beinn a' Chrulaiste over Rannoch Moor.

A detail to delight up on the moor.

*Landmark Blackrock with the
Buachaille behind.*

Ancient staging post and milestone on the Way Way, the Kingshouse Hotel.

Buachaille Etive Mor.

The Sisters of Glencoe.

The secretive Grey Mare's Tail at Kinlochleven.

One of the more unusual plants flowering on Rannoch Moor.

The Pap of Glencoe from the ascent above Kinlochleven.

Heading into the Lairig Mor.

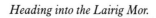

Striding out: above Kinlochleven.

Ben Nevis in sight – the climax of the walk.

Overleaf: *Whence we have come: looking south from the summit of Ben Nevis.*

champagne ready in a cooler. Standing beside this spread was a waiter in full rig of black tails and bow tie and an attractive girl in French folk costume.

Dave was the first to gather his wits.

'Expectin us, wis youse?'

The 'waiter's' explanation was given in good Glasgow accents which, briefly, added to the unreality. They were brother and sister and their parents were both celebrating their sixtieth birthdays that week – and marking the occasion by walking the West Highland Way.

'We thoucht we'd gie them a wee surprise.'

'Weel, you gied us a big yin.'

Beinn Dorain kept its cone profile for the gentle walk down to the Auch Gleann, the glen that moats the mountain. The West Highland railway ran a score across the foot of Beinn Dorain, a straight line that made it look as if someone had sawed through the mountain, so that it could be lifted off like the cover of a tagine. Slabs of conifer plantations lay in the valley. The stream at their feet fell away in the sort of tight wiggles a skier would be happy to track down a slalom course. Specky was clicking away.

'Have you finished yet?' Dave demanded. 'The midges is eating me.'

Specky replied, 'On you go, I'll catch up.'

Some people will do anything for a photograph.

Auch has the same odd feeling of spaciousness as Dalrigh, which simply emphasised the steepnesses around. A curlew glided past, trailing its weird wailing cry, emphasising the emptiness.

Tyndrum to Bridge of Orchy still has the straightforward feel of a military road. Wade's surveyor, and then successor, William Caulfeild,[12] was to build a greater mileage of roads but is given much less credit. The fine arch of bridge over the River Orchy is his work.

As they angled towards the railway Specky recounted a tale about the line.

'Last century they ran an early morning "ghost train" as they called it, from Glasgow to Fort William, a goods, so the guard could, and did, often take a nap, quite legally. After Bridge of Orchy the line makes a long, long ascent across Rannoch Moor to Corrour and the guard went off to sleep. At Corrour, the jerking either loosened or broke a coupling which detached the guard's van and while the train went off down for Loch Treig the guard's van began to roll back the way. They saw it coming at Rannoch and the rules said they should turn any runaway onto a siding and let it hit the buffers. Instead of probably killing the guard they let the van through. So did Gorton. After twenty-three miles of freewheeling it went through Bridge of Orchy. There they knew it wouldn't go much further because of the hill, and further on a bit the van lost momentum, stopped, and then rolled gently back into Bridge of Orchy station. The stopping probably woke up the guard, who stuck his head out – and was decidedly nonplussed to find himself at Bridge of Orchy.'

'He wis lucky,' Dave commented. 'Somethin like that happened at Achnashellach. The engine became loose an' when the driver at last had a keek he fun he didna hae ony coaches. Do you know what the stupid f...er did?'

'No.'

'He gangs back *up* the line tae find them. An he did – bang!'

About a mile before the station they could see a huge boulder sitting on the hillside, obviously fallen from high on Beinn Dorain. Clach a' Bhein (*stone of the hill*) in Victorian times was romanticised as Rob Roy's Putting Stone! A man was sitting with his rucksack at the stone.

'Heading for Fort William?' Hector asked.

'No; just here. I was waiting for someone to come along in order to get a photo of Willie and me.'

'Is Willie coming soon, then?'

'Oh, he's here.'

Dave was framing an 'Oh, aye!', he later confessed, but the man had pulled out an urn from his rucker.

'His ashes.'

Specky naturally volunteered to take the photo with the man's camera and had him pose against the rock with the urn. Cloud had come down on the summit.

Handing the camera back, Specky asked, 'Good friend of yours?'

'Best friend I ever had.'

'Where was he from? You sound from down south.'

'Oh, Willie lived with me. Never apart. Even in bed.'

This was rather startling. Dave had already made some rough – unrepeatable – observations about two lads at Crianlarich he'd decided were gay.

'He did get past two hundred Munros. Sad not to complete.'

They nodded. Well …

'Still, he did live till he was sixteen.'

Dave audibly choked. Specky thought he had maybe meant 'sixty'.

'Best dog I ever had.'

They clattered through the underpass at the station, and curved down to cross the A82 to the hotel, where they had left provisions. The bar called. A pint or three later they were standing on the humped bridge when a group of laden Way Way walkers scurried past them without a greeting, which was most unusual. After loud discussions the noisy group headed off up through the trees where the Way dutifully follows the old military road over the Mam Carraigh, eleven contour lines of up-just-to-come-down, as they'd noted in the hotel. As the path was likely to be boggy, and there would be no view to reward the toil, and there were these yahoos ahead, the decision to go round rather than over was easily made. They'd just set off when Dave stopped.

'F...in eejits!'

'Who?'

'Us. Our food fir the next twa days!'

'I'll go,' Hector said. 'I left it and know who will fetch it.'

Specky, muttering about the flat light, took several shots of the pleasing span; like so many of the military road bridges it combined simplicity and grace. The far bank was bright with meadowsweet and yellow monkey flowers. Hector returned with two carrier bags of goodies and a load of beer, which he divided before their keen gaze. The division seemed fair.

A few big drops of rain polka-dotted the road as they set off. There were a couple of tents beside the wide River Orchy. The figure coming up with water to one tent wore a veil and they caught a whiff of a mosquito coil burning. 'No takin ony chances.' With the cloud level dropping and the atmosphere muggy, the midges could well be bad that evening, but neither midges nor rain then came to much and a wee breeze soon removed the raindrop pattern from the road and the midges from the air. The first rather featureless mile went past to singing about three-quarters of the verses they could recall of the 'Bonnie Lass o Fyvie, O'. Before Caulfeild's soldiers built the military road, travellers went on by Achallader to ford the Water of Tulla, a lesser obstacle than the rush of Orchy. The modern A82 came in the early 1930s and was described as an intrusive eyesore by those opposing its construction – a road which is so taken for granted these days.

'It was a magnificent piece of engineering,' Specky said, 'Years ahead of common practice. Apart from having to strengthen bridges for today's juggernauts, hardly anything has had to be done.'

They were aware of a group of walkers ahead, on the road like themselves, and over a mile slipped past before they caught up on a family group. Mother, and what could have been twins (boy and girl), were redheads, with remarkably similar features, but it was the father who caught their interest as he had a harnessed Golden Labrador leading him along. He was blind. The boy, in ringing tones, informed the man, 'Hey, dad, one of them has a red brolly with penguins on it.' Dave winced but Hector just smiled. The two parties chatted a bit. The family were from near Durham. They'd done the Speyside Way the year before. 'My sister is giving us support,' the man said. 'We'll be at the Inveroran tonight.'

'Might see you, then.'

Our trio slowly drew ahead, until the damp woodlands muffled off the piping voices of the youngsters.

'Doire Darach, that name again', though not *oakwoods* at all but a surviving, and living piece of the old pine woods that once covered the Highlands as far north as the rough reaches of Loch Maree and ran from Argyll to the Cairngorms.

'You know, walkers would be the first to complain if we went back to a natural landscape. Just look at it.'

'It's quite splendid, Hector.'

'Yes. But could you imagine Munro-bagging if it was all as wild and overgrown as this? You'd need a machete, not a Leki pole.'

The American author Nathaniel Hawthorne ran into weather he described as 'a drizzle … of such minute drops that they had not weight enough to fall … genuine Scotch mist'. (He added, 'It is well enough to have experienced it, though I would willingly never see it again.') Specky recalled this description as they neared Inveroran, for they walked in a smirr that meant they didn't want to stop to don waterproofs but were being fine sprayed without their protection. So they hurried, which just made them hot and sweaty.

Inveroran is just how imagination sees an old drovers' inn, a trim, clean-lined building sitting as comfortably as a mushroom in the cup of the hills. There are no concrete wings, or brash conservatories wounding the old body.

Cattle being driven to the south in droving days only progressed about a dozen miles a day, their stopping places still marked all unconsciously by Way Way walkers. (Inveroran, Inverarnan, Tyndrum were all 'stances', as were Kingshouse and Altnafeadh.) Eight thousand beasts often began their journeys by swimming the Sound of Sleat from Skye at Kylerhea. Roads hardly existed and when they did the unwieldy beasts were tipped over to have their hooves shod. Even geese being marched to market would have their feet tarred. Every burn could be a hazard in spate and every walker is all too aware of what cows' feet can do to damp ground. The drovers often slept in the open, living largely on oatmeal, and only too glad when there was some sort of shelter, such as Inveroran.

One of the amazing aspects concerns their dogs. Once the drover had delivered his beasts, he'd often stay on to do seasonal work – and he'd send his dog home alone, sometimes the length of England. The dogs would get food at the inns and the drover would settle the bill on his return later.

They had an hour in the bar and made the most of it, being joined by a couple, Brian and Margaret (they never learned their surname) who came from Glenageary, south of Dublin. They were keen Munroists and had been away out to the hills beyond Loch Dochard. 'Ben of Agony' they suggested as a pronunciation for Beinn nan Aighenan.

'We ran out of steam on Meall nan Eun. But we'll do Stob Ghabhar and Stob a' Choire Odhair tomorrow.'

'Weather permitting,' Margaret added, looking at the weeping windows. Batteries of wind were now firing salvos of rain from the west.

'Aye, weather permittin.'

'You staying here?' Brian asked.

'No, Clachgour.'

'That the tiny hut along from Victoria Bridge?'

'Yes.'

'But we're dining here first. We get quite enough of Hector's cooking.'

'Gawd, Specky! Dinna say things like that. He might gang on strike.'

'Just joking. We're all of Napoleon's opinion about what an army does with its stomach. So we take every care of ours.'

'Where's your next stop?' Hector asked.

'Kingshouse,' Brian replied. 'I'm afraid we're taking the option of a solid roof every night. We likes our comforts. Taking in some mountains, though. You climbed anything?'

'Ben Lomond and Ben Challum.'

'Oh, we did Ben Lomond too, and great days from Crianlarich, and the Lui group from Tyndrum. The weather's been quite kind. We've had some disaster trips to Scotland. Skye usually. One trip to Skye we climbed all the Munros in the Cairngorms.'

That sounded very Irish.

'Eh?'

'Jesus, after three days of non-stop deluge we'd had enough of Skye so we drove across from Skye to the 'Gorms – and they were great.'

They went on to talk about how much more attractive it was to be car-free on something like the Way Way and how much could be done without even owning a vehicle. Brian mentioned an Edinburgh friend who owned no car, had recently completed his Munros, and claimed he had more than halved the price per Munro by not being a car owner.

'That was one of the ideas behind the TGO Challenge,' Margaret said. 'Get away from the car. Make people spend locally. Make them stay locally. Meet locals. May was chosen to catch better weather, few midges and B&Bs glad of extra custom before the busy season.'

'You've done some crossings, Hector.' Brian said, 'Ever gone up Loch Ericht to Dalwhinnie?'

'You can hardly *not*, some time. Yes.'

'We met the keeper from Ben Alder. Geordie Oswald. We could hardly get away from him. He said he did road repairs then, so he could have a chat with the 'hikers'. Said he knew when they were coming. "First it's the cuckoos, then it's the hikers." Great chap, so he was.'

They nodded. Geordie had now retired. Specky then said, 'Thinking of Loch Ericht, and the use of trains, there's a startling story in an early SMC Journal about a meet at the inn here.[13] Two members came *via Dalwhinnie*: Naismith and Gilbert Thomson. They got off a train from Glasgow at half past three in the morning and were here for dinner that night, having walked down Loch Ericht and right across Rannoch Moor.'

'How far was that?'

'Forty miles at least.'

'You'd be hard put to equal that today.'

'Aye, so ye wid. There's nae trains stop at Dalwhinnie noo.'[14]

They were called in for dinner and ran their tables together. The room was small and cosy. The family with the blind father was sitting by the window. They all said hello in passing. On the walls there were Landseer-like prints of stags with attitudes, pictures of the inn in olden times and a photo of a white-bearded Victorian ghillie holding a whopping big salmon. Years ago, the waitress said, there was a framed quote from Dorothy Wordsworth's 1803 journal, when she and William had stopped for breakfast, 'the butter not eatable, the barley-cakes fusty, the oat-bread so hard I could not chew it, and there were only four eggs, which they had boiled as hard as stones'. It got stolen.

'Last time I dined here,' Hector said, 'was to celebrate an old school friend's final Munro. Beinn na Lap. So we had the pleasure of the train across the Moor from Bridge of Orchy. Last Munros are becoming quite celebratory affairs these days. Couple of years before, I had one at the Kingshouse, after a soaking on Stob a' Choire Odhair, and the girl's brother worked for Brocks so he laid on fireworks that night. He warned the police, let me say. He invited people from the hotel and the bar to come out and watch but nobody was very interested – probably thought it would just be a garden November the fifth sort of thing. The first big bang shook the hotel. Everyone came out. They thought they'd been bombed.'

There was a lot more chat about the West Highland Way, Munros, midges, and earlier travellers. Hector, who had inherited a set of the SMC Journals, asked if they knew about the fiasco by engineers surveying Rannoch Moor for the railway. Two early numbers described what could have been a tragedy. He told the story as he remembered it, how seven engineers and others involved in the railway crossed the Moor in winter, became lost and had all sorts of misadventures before reaching Inveroran with a blizzard starting. He got some details wrong and forgot parts, so the story is given fully in Appendix 3, rather than a garbled version here.

At the end of this tale the family at the window rose to go. The man paused to say, 'We couldn't help listening to your story. A good bedtime one for the kids.' The twins grinned and said cheery goodnights.

They went out and Dave turned to Brian and Margaret.

'Would you hae kent he wis blin?'

Brian and Margaret agreed to call in at Clachgour so they could all do Stob Ghabhar together – if the weather improved. The trio left in a steady drizzle, clad in waterproof tops and bottoms.

There were tents scattered along this most unlikely of A roads (A8005). They had to stop their chattering ('Duncan Bàn was born up there'), as one tent by the Gleann Fuar bridge had a trannie going full blast and Pink Floyd full blast would make Stob Ghabhar cower.

'That's them we saw heading over the hill.'

As the *boom boom* beat died away behind them Dave said something blunt and to the point that music on the Way Way was best kept to oneself.

Loch Tulla was the colour of setting concrete.

'Shame! I love this corner,' Specky said. 'Used to come to Clachgour quite often.'

So in gloomy dusk they walked over Victoria Bridge and turned up the stony track for Clachgour, the pines whining with a strengthening wind, like dogs on a leash.

'Lucky Brian an Margaret,' Dave muttered as he sucked wet off the cord of his hood.

They had taken Specky's description of the GUM Club's Clachgour Hut being little more than a garden shed with a pinch of salt. Once he'd unlocked the door and taken down the shutters they believed him. The building was simply a corrugated iron box (once a school) with a strengthened ceiling to act as a sleeping platform. Six would cover the space available, with one sleeper facing the quite real possibility of going down the hole for the ladder during the night. Facing the door was a table with a window above it. As the ceiling cut across the window another rectangle had been cut out of the ceiling's sleeping floor to allow the top of the window to open on a central ratchet. There was 'an outside loo', Specky had said. When Dave asked where, Specky gave a wave of his hand round the landscape. Water came from the burn. Cooking and lighting was with gas.

As they sat listening to the rain drumming on the roof they blessed Specky's idea of using the hut. He told them endless stories of goings-on there when he was a student. According to him, thirty-five had once fitted in for a night. (Bob Aitken's guidebook comment on this was that the Black Hole of Calcutta must have been pleasanter.) On one meet they found a member missing when they woke in the morning. His sleeping bag was there. And so were his clothes. *That* caused a panic. Had the silly bugger gone for a swim and drowned himself? They dressed hurriedly and had just left the hut when they saw their mate walking down the Allt Toaig path, starkers. He apologised: 'I'm apt to go sleepwalking.' They threatened to belay him the next night. On one occasion the door had been left open and a stag got in and then panicked. From above they watched the beast trash the place.

They finished off their cache bottle of Cabernet Sauvignon and took themselves up to the loft. The rain sounded harder (and wetter) from their perch up in the gods and the tin shack made an echo chamber for Dave's snoring. Specky took a pill.

Chapter 9

It sometimes rains

The Irish couple did not show up in the morning, nor were the trio averse to 'sleeping it out', for the rain it rained. Bad-tempered rain.

'Have you no a f...in quote fir it?' Dave asked, nursing his tea, and his headache.

Specky obliged.

'"Hey, ho, the wind and the rain ... For the rain it raineth every day." Shakespeare. *Twelfth Night*, I think.'

'I thought it was *Lear*,' said Hector.

They argued this with some frustration. Clachgour, however, did not hold the *Works of William Shakespeare* to settle the argument.

They tried to read: Aitken, the hut book, the books they'd carried (largely unread till then), but you can't settle in those circumstances. They brewed and had an early lunch – and went. Later they would think how silly they had been to go on. They could easily have had another night at Clachgour. They were not pushed for time; perhaps just not long enough on the trail to go at the trail's acceptable pace.

The pines at Forest Lodge were sizzling in the rain and the wind sounded like a cat-fight in the bushes. Every now and then a big gust would clear the trees, like a dog shaking its coat, and willywaws would skitter along the wet road and the grass slopes would fluster and flurry.

The West Highland Way signs pointed along what was the old Glen Coe road (the Caulfeild road went along on a higher line) and this led up and round steadily, soon leaving the Blackmount trees for the wetter wet of higher ground. Every now and then storms came rolling down the slopes off Stob Ghabhar and Clachlet. They crossed the wandering watershed again.[15]

The view over the Moor was depressing, the landscape sprawled with an oily sort of brownness, like one of those crinkly-leaved salads, the lochs the colour and look of cucumber slices. It's an odd place, for all the waters from the slopes of the Way run across the Moor eastwards, the start of the vast Rannoch–Tummel–Tay drainage which creates the largest volume of water entering the sea from any British river. Yet, ahead, just round these hills Glen Etive runs down to the western sea, no distance away. And then again, far east over the Moor were the springs that fed the Water of Tulla which flowed west to join the Orchy, Loch Awe and the Atlantic.

Hector walked smugly with the penguin brolly over his shoulder, changing hands or shoulder as wind and route varied. He had his hood off and jacket half open down the front, whereas Dave and Specky were cocooned in their jackets, hoods up. Gore-Tex or not, they felt claustrophobic. And nothing stops the ultimate crepitation of wet.

Hector commented that Rannoch Moor was nothing but a wet desert.

'A pretty good description,' Specky said. 'The word comes from the Latin *desere* which means to abandon or forsake.' He wiped his specs for the umpteenth time.

'Godforsaken, ah'd ca it.'

They traichled on, the track crossing the discouraging reach called 'The Moss' on the map, but it didn't appear any wetter than anything else. Six stags, antlers half grown or in velvet, cantered onto and along the track, almost invisible within their explosive clouds of spray. The normal nodding heads of bog cotton hung in sodden stillness, as attractive as discarded hospital swabs.

'Ba bridge, at last!' Hector said as the birch-hidden feature neared.

'Ba-ba-bridge,' Dave bleated.

There's an impressive length of the original cobbling down to the bridge, a simple span, with no parapet, arching over a deep cutting of river which was racing through, beer-coloured and with a foaming head.

Despite the wet Specky went down the river a bit to try and photograph the bridge. Descending the muddy bank, he went for a slide, arms flailing and body twisting in a painful effort not to sit down or see his camera fly into the surge and froth of the river. Looking up to the bridge, he waved the miserable-looking figures aside so they were masked by the shivering birch trees. Even at that close distance, all detail was lost and background non-existent, so he studied some ragged lines of rocks, like crocodile teeth, that were being well flossed by the spate. Dave encouraged him with 'F...in urry up!'

Dave also took photos but mainly of abstract shapes and textures that appealed and gave ideas for his work. Today his camera remained in a poly bag inside his rucker. Hector didn't carry a camera, declaring he preferred to see the world whole and not in little rectangles.

'See him up there,' Dave said. 'If he created rain could he no hae organised the distribution a bitty better?'

A couple passed them, so defended against the weather that all they could see were eyes peering from the dark caves of their waterproof hoods. The nearest raised a hand in greeting *en passant*. Hector just said 'Aye', conditions hardly encouraging a conversation. The couple swished on, feet splashing in the flowing path. Ba Bridge might as well not have existed for them.

Dave, who had his head under Hector's brolly, said, 'Dae you mind yon mannie in the suit – at Milngavie an Rowardennan?' Hector nodded. 'Dae you think he's really daein the Wey Wey?' Hector shrugged. 'Ah mean, he'd be droukit; imagine him in this.' They did. They would recall the figure several times during their walk and mentioned him once or twice to other Way Way walkers but nobody else seemed to have encountered the man. By the end they half-doubted their own recollections. A suit on the Way Way!?

This stretch of military road, from Inveroran to Kingshouse, was built in little more than a single season, though it took the bribe of extra pay and a total force of a thousand soldiers, working from both ends, to succeed. There were no JCBs in those days. The soldiers' tents rotted in the wet, completed work was washed out, providing food was a nightmare. As Dave would comment back in Fife, 'An we thocht we had it bad.'

Another small plantation, the barely visible ruin of Ba Cottage ('fancy living there?'), a path off along to the A82 and Loch Ba, the military road doing another break 'off and at em' uphill, a cairn up on the skyline ... the eye devoured any little detail as if they'd been precious shells found on an empty strand.

' "Hey, ho, the wind and the rain ... For the rain it raineth every day." ' Specky warbled out his Shakespeare again and the argument with Hector was briefly resumed. Specky worked next door to the library in Kirkcaldy so he checked once back home.

Dave stomped along, almost delighting in sloshing through the wettest places. If you are not heading for hypothermia because of cold there comes a stage when wetness can almost become enjoyable in itself.

'We do have waterproof skins,' Specky had said earlier. 'Though I feel washed to the bone.'

'Pity we have to have this soaker *now*. This was where we decided to do the Way Way.'

Dave shook a drip off his nose.

'Aye. But at least there's nae midges. The buggers is aw drooned.'

'A book I was reading said they don't like wind, or bright sunlight and' (Specky paused for effect) 'you never get them above ten thousand feet.'

'Thank God fir that. Could you imagine a transatlantic flight wi the cabin fu o midges?'

They squelched along in silence awhile. Dave gave a snigger.

'I've just foon win thing wrang wi ma guid new bits. Maybe they dinna let water in but, by f...!, they let it oot. Look!'

They stopped and looked at Dave's feet. He wiggled his toes and bubbles fizzed out of his lace holes.

'Ah didna rinse ma socks verra weel, did ah?'

'Well, you are now.'

They paused near the summit of the track ('At last!') to have a bite to eat and drink. Specky sat on a knoll, the others stood, 'erse intae wund, like sheep'.

'That cairn up there is a memorial to Peter Fleming. "Author, Soldier and Traveller", it says.'

Blackmount is the banking family's estate and Peter, up on this brae, with its grand view over Rannoch Moor ('well, sometimes') had had a fatal heart attack.

'Guid way tae gang.'

'His brother Ian was much more famous, of course, for he was the creator of James Bond, 007 and all that.'

'What a screwy contrast of brothers they must have been.'

'There's another book, all about here, you must read,' Specky said, 'called, if I'm right, *The High Tops of Black Mount*. Written by a woman, the Marchioness of Breadalbane. They owned all this here and right round and down Glen Etive. I don't know about him but she was a fanatical deer stalker – and you should see the pictures of her in ankle-length skirts. Imagine that, *here*.'

'Imagine that, *now*!' Hector twirled his brolly.

'On one occasion she went this way and down Glen Etive, stayed a night in a cottage or bothy, went down the loch for the next night and home by Glen Kinglass, and Clashgour, an "easy" alternative because she couldn't go stalking.'

'So much for downtrodden Victorian women.'

'Come on, the LSCC[16] was formed in 1908. The marchioness was made the club's first honorary president. Blackrock's the club's hut.'

'Ah ken.'

They walked on. Dave was humming to himself. He stopped and looked about at the desolation.

'Ma Gawd! This wid be a guid place tae dee in.'

'You that bad?'

'No. The opposite, ya tumshie. Ah like it! Even when it's pissin doon. There's aye a sunny side tae rain.'

Hector grinned. 'My will specifies my ashes are to be spread on Rannoch Moor. By the Rannoch Rowan.'

'Whit's that?'

'When you drive up onto the Moor from Loch Tulla there's a rowan growing out a split rock, on the left, the only tree in miles – till they planted conifers over the way – so that's where I'll end. Never pass without giving it a wave.'

'Cheery bugger, you.'

'No more than you and your comment. That tree's always been my "Welcome!" to the hills, ever since I parked my bike as a laddie and sat on top of the rock to ... to worship. As good a word as any.'

'Aye.' Then Dave smiled. 'Wid you mind if ah jined ye? Ma ashes ah mean.'

The track began to dip, as if tired of fighting hills and rain. Specky asked, 'What day of the week is it?'

After a bit of calculating they decided it was Tuesday. 'Why?'

'If it had been the weekend there might have been a club using Blackrock. We might still be lucky. After all we are members of a very respectable club. We might get in.'

The very thought lengthened their stride down the rough track. They could see the cottage and the ski facilities and the big, bold, black Buachaille glared across the Moor at them. Every slope was laced with white threads of spate waters.

'Skied here, Specky?'

'Yes. Cracked two ribs on one visit.'

'How?'

'Near whiteout and I shot into the well-named Haggis Trap. I landed on my chest. Not amusing. Couldn't laugh for weeks.'

Specky let the others walk on ahead a moment while he sloped off behind some boulders for a pee. ('Why don't overtrousers have flies?') He immediately let out a vigorous yelp.

Both Hector and Dave turned to see him going, in Dave's brief phraseology, 'erse over tit'. They thought this quite an amusing spectacle but Specky wailed, 'I've dropped my glasses. Help me find them, you bastards.' Dave hauled Specky upright ('He wis lying waving his feet in the air like a tortoise') and Hector picked up the, mercifully unbroken, spectacles without which the poor lad could hardly see. He'd meant to bring spares.

'I tripped.'

'Aye.'

And simultaneously they all saw what he had tripped on: a fine head of antlers which belonged to a dead stag. A very dead stag.

'Ach, it couldna hae been you smellin like that.'

Specky regarded the antlers that had fankled him so effectively. 'Twelve tines!' he cried. 'A royal. I'll take them.'

This was easier said than done. Tugging was ineffectual and so was jumping on them. Even pounding with boulders simply shattered the skull to release decayed matter with a smell that was indescribably foul.

'Glad Whisky's no here; the f...er wid roll in it.'

'Could do with a hacksaw.'

'Ah can len ye ma Swiss Army knife.'

Specky was not amused. He perched the trophy across two boulders and they all added their weight. Apart from practically demolishing the skull (and adding the stench to their boots) they were no nearer snapping off the antlers from the pedicles.

'And to think, in the autumn, they just loosen and fall off by themselves,' Hector commented.

'Leave the f...ers. Come back efter.'

Specky hid the antlers and they went on.

'One wey o warmin up.'

Sadly, as Specky had rather expected, Blackrock was not in use. They tried every door. Sleeping in the coal cellar would have done fine.

'We should have organised a key.'

'Fairly good ground here. Let's just pitch.'

'What? On the doorstep? I don't think it's allowed.'

'Hell wi that. This is a matter o survival. Wha's goin tae mind onywey?'

So they pitched on top of the bank facing the front door. Waterproofs were peeled off.

'Ma jaickit pocket's fu o water!' Dave complained. 'Aw yon modern technology an ye hae pockets fu o water. An can they nae sort oot waterproof ruckers? The best bit o gear ah've got is the poly bag inside ma rucker – heavy gauge frae the Fife Buildin Supply Company.'

'At least we're reasonably dry underneath.'

'I think it was Billy Connolly who said, "There's no such thing as bad weather – only the wrong clothes." '

'Away ben, youse twa. I'll fetch the water.'

They looked round. The swaying heather made the cottage feel like a ship ploughing the Minch. They climbed into their storm-tossed life raft.

When Dave was scrambling into the tent Specky shouted, 'Hey! Look out for that flower. Don't harm it. It eats midges.'

'Oh, aye,' Dave replied but he avoided the butterwort and was interested enough in hearing the veracity of Specky's claim. Anything that ate midges was a friend.

Specky had been to Iceland and couldn't resist the opening. 'You know, Dave, in Iceland the midges are so bad that I once saw cows wearing trusses to protect their udders. Cows with bras on.'

Dave duly snorted, 'An I've seen tin spiders walkin on brass legs.'

'Honest, Dave. The midges there come in waves so numerous that when they die the ground receives layer on layer of bodies. This nitrogen enriches the grass so it grows lush and the cows produce huge quantities of milk, so much milk they have to wear girdle things to keep their udders from hitting the ground. Cows with bras.'

Dave wasn't sure. You never could tell with Specky.

'Pass me a bottle,' he demanded. (They'd carried *bottles* of Red Cuillin all the way from Bridge of Orchy – a purchase made earlier in Nevisport.)

They were a bit more efficient at pitching the tent this time, despite hurrying. They supped the welcome ale and then equally welcome tea. 'Surprising how drouthy you can become, even in the wet,' Hector said. 'So what do you fancy for supper?'

'Whit aboot a steak? Rare. Wi tartare sauce. An chips.'

'Far too early. Let's finish the cake, though.'

'It's for tomorrow.'

'Blow tomorrow. Today is today.'

The rain came and went, slowly moderating, as if growing weak from its exertions, and dusk ushered in a strange quiet where the only continuo was the gentle, varying notes of water flowing.

'"For the curse of water has come again because of the wrath of God." That's Chesterton. "The water has drowned the Matterhorn as deep as a Mendip mine / But I don't care where the water goes if it doesn't get into the wine."'

'We're OK then. We've nae wine.'

'I remember a holiday on a wine place in South Africa,' Hector sighed. 'Plenty of sun. Maybe rains a dozen days in the year. You get so used to sun. Growing up in South Africa I was outdoors all the time, running barefoot with Zulu friends in the Valley of a Thousand Hills. Scotland was quite a shock, I can tell you, both for its climate and school. School was like a prison. Thank God the Ochils were there at least – though once they landed me in trouble.

'I woke one glorious sunny morning, took one look at the hills and was off. Left a note for granny. I was way beyond White Wisp when I remembered I was supposed to be playing in a rugger match that day. Oh God, I never heard the end of it. "Letting the side down, Macdonald. Ya! Ya! Ya!"'

'You ken, Hector, I almaist feel sorry fir yir teachers. Ah thocht ah wis a hard case.'

'You probably both were,' Specky said, but he had been like blotting paper at school, absorbing everything.

They cooked a good meal, even if not to Dave's dream specifications. As usual too, in Specky's words, they had it 'backwards'. On arrival they had soaked apple rings in their one big pot. These had swelled so they added a little sugar and boiled them up. They swelled some more so the lid was lifted up and had to have a chunk of granite placed on top to hold it down. The juice then bubbled out. So, once a packet of instant custard had been stirred in, they ate the apples. The dixie was topped up to cook some rice, with some caraway seed sprinkled in at the last moment. Into this was added a chopped up tin of ham, an onion and a couple of tomatoes. (The tomatoes had been safe inside the pot while they were walking.) Lastly, the dixie was used for soup. In that order, Hector preached, you never needed to wash the pan till the end. 'I wouldn't fancy apples after a curry.' Coffee and biscuits finished off the repast.

'Par for the course,' said Specky.

'No bad,' said Dave, praise indeed.

'Not exactly a strenuous day.'

'Ten miles maybe.'

'Och weel, it's ten mair miles nearer the Fort.'

'If weather has to be bad, really bad is more interesting.'

No doubt the rain was giving the stars a good wash but they still couldn't reach the borders of sleep. Nobody was really tired though faces glowed from the weather's beating.

'For goodness sake, Dave, stop wriggling.'

'There's a bloody stane under ma back.'

'Then sort it.' Hector's tone had just a touch of happy smugness. (A neighbour's unhappiness is easily borne.)

There was silence and stillness for a few minutes. Hector and Specky edged towards sleep, to the continuing lullaby of rain, then Dave gave another of his heaves. They were all wide awake again. Specky sniggered.

'F... you!' Dave yelled and heaved himself out of his sleeping bag and, of course, in such circumstances, his sheet liner did a Laocoön performance to strangle him. His language deteriorated as he thrust bare feet into cold, dank boots and went out into the unfriendly night.

'Roll over, Specky,' Hector pleaded.

Dave didn't so much reach under the groundsheet as start a mammoth excavation to 'howk' out the offending stone.

'You'd think he was underneath.'

'Ah am!' came a muffled cry.

Eventually a rather drookit Dave crawled back in, borrowed their one towel for a cursory wipe, slipped off his now soaked briefs and fought his way back into his sleeping bag. After some dog-like movement he sighed and all was still again.

Hector's breathing had reached a deepening rhythm that kept Specky listening instead of following suit, when there was another almighty heave from Dave, which rolled Hector back onto Specky. Hector choked on his breath. 'What the hell?' he muttered, surfacing to the claustrophobic reality.

'Ah canna sleep,' Dave girned. 'There's a f...in big hole under me noo.'

Chapter 10

Devil's Staircase

No tap-dancing rain on the tent, anyway; however, extended bladders rather than enthusiasm had them up and doing.

'Ma back's sair,' Dave girned.

'Hey! We're onto the last map today,' Specky noted as he spooned his warming porridge.

'How far to Kinlochleven?'

'About ten miles, but over the Devil's Staircase, the highest point on the whole trip.'

'How do you feel about a B&B tonight, then?'

'If we've a fecht aw day wi rain, I'd no mind. Or the bunkhoose.'

Specky nodded.

That decision seemed to improve spirits, if not weather, and they were soon pulling on damp boots on top of damp stockings. Specky's 'An excellent day for not climbing anything' didn't call for any disagreement. They shared communal items: Specky the flysheet and poles, Dave the tent and pegs while Hector had stove, pan and some food. When it came to weight they were as canny as brothers watching the division of a cake. Specky bundled away the sopping flysheet, thinking it was several pounds heavier. Dave used a stone to straighten out some of the tent pegs. They all giggled at this operation, being more used to seeing Dave using a great hammer on red-hot metal.

'As well being off early,' Hector said.

'Aye, the midges don't like this raw cold.'

They had only gone down the road a few minutes when there was the now recognisable pong of something dead and decaying. Dave trauchled through the heather, hoping to lay claim to a set of antlers. He suddenly stopped, grimaced, and came back, swearing steadily.

'Dinna gang ower. It's a deid hind, wi a hauf-born calf hangin oot o her.'

At the A82, Dave, who at the planning stage had had every intention of making use of the Kingshouse in the evening, now argued that they could lop off some miles by not going there at all. 'Dae you mind? At this time o morning the A82 widna be busy. We could nip doon an alang tae Altnafeadh in hauf the time. Be in Kinlochleven for opening time.'

Nobody argued much. Principles are fine – in good weather.

Later, they decided this was another mistake. Main roads are *never* a better option. What traffic there was seemed to take delight in spraying them with dirty water. A lorry passing turned Hector's brolly outside in. He'd put it up to try and dry it off. Dave used a range of blunt Anglo-Saxon. At least the road went steadily downhill to the white concrete arches of the bridge – so often used as a postcard foreground in pictures of the Buachaille Etive Mor (*the big shepherd of Etive*), which was having something of an argument with the bullying clouds. Such of the peak as they could see was shiny wet, black and seamed with silvery falls. Past the Glen Etive road end they went down to walk along the banks of the Coupall, the river that drains this mountain of mountains. On the other side was Jacksonville, the DIY hut of the Creag Dhu, quite unreachable, the stepping stones invisible below the brown tide of water. One guidebook declares that the route by the Coupall 'is not waymarked and is rough, trackless and not recommended'. Sometimes not knowing too much can be an advantage.

'We could have gone to *stay* at the Kingshouse last night,' Hector suddenly said.

'Never thought about it. Must have been really set in camping mode.'

'Wir brains wis waterlogged.'

Specky said, 'I stayed there once. The views from the lounge window are magnificent. On the windowsills there are wee brass plates naming the views as if they were pictures. Horatio McCulloch sort of views.'

'I've stayed there too,' said Hector. 'Heard a story about the place. Back in the days of droving, two homing drovers arrived at the pre-military Kingshouse and, there only being a lassie in the place, they were directed to a nearby barn for the night. Next day they took farewell of the bonnie lass and headed for the Devil's Staircase. Many months later one of them received a letter from the said lassie saying that she was pregnant. He at once went over to the next glen to confront his mate.

'"You remember our night in the barn at Kingshouse?"

'"Aye."

'"Did you by any chance go a-wandering in the night?"

'"I might have."

'"And did you give the lassie *my* name and address?"

'"More than likely."

'They rather fell out over this and both wrote their complaints. When they met some months later, the original victim, still irate, demanded if his companion had done the right thing.

'"Oh, aye."

'"And what has happened?"

'"Oh man, you'll no believe it. The lassie deid and I've inherited the Kingshouse. Got a braw wee laddie too."'

The clouds were billowing out of the Glen Coe gap and along the slopes they would soon be tackling. They were quite glad not to be descending the glen, recalling Charles Dickens' description of it in 1841. 'Glencoe itself is perfectly *terrible*. The pass is an awful place. It is shut in on each side by enormous rocks from which great torrents come rushing down in all directions ... there are scores of glens, high up, which form such haunts as you might imagine yourself wandering in, in the very light and madness of a fever. The very recollection makes one shudder ...'. The Reverend John Lettice from Sussex described the Moor in 1792 as 'an immense vacuity', in which there was 'nothing to contemplate, ... unless numberless mis-shapen blocks of stone rising hideously above the surface of the earth, could be said to contradict the inanity of our prospects'.

Dave's description was briefer, 'Gey dreich.'

To be fair, Dickens went on to say, 'This is a wondrous region. The way the mists were stalking about today, and the clouds lying upon the hills; the deep glens, the high rocks, the rushing waterfalls and the roaring rivers in deep gulfs below; were all stupendous' – which might have described the BFs' day.

Hector brought up something else. 'My father remembers this road being built. The "new road", he always called it. But with typical governmental crassness the road was opened by a Campbell. OK, this was Sir Malcolm Campbell, the land and sea record holder, but still ...'

Prospects improved for the Fifers and, extraordinarily quickly, the weather changed and with it their mood. By Altnafeadh the day had transformed. The Buachaille still bulked big and black and the wee cottage of Lagangarbh (an SMC hut) looked white enough to be used in a soap powder commercial. Everything, of course, had been well washed. The sensible thing was to nip over the Devil's Staircase and let nature get on with her spin drying. So they didn't.

Hector, while giving the impression of laziness, was never one to pass up an opportunity.

'We could do Beinn a' Chrulaiste,' he proposed.

'I tak it that's a hill an no a kindie gargle.'

'That one. Dead easy. A Corbett.'

Dave was about to reply about folk who ticked hills but then reconsidered. A tick is a tick is a tick. And at least Hector wasn't suggesting the Buachaille. Some day he too might be leaning on the Corbetts, so having one in the bag would do no harm. As long as some silly bugger didn't go and promote it or demote it or whatever. On the other hand they wouldn't reach Kinlochleven till the afternoon. The Corbett, which he wasn't even going to try and pronounce, would cost a pint or three.

'Gawd, the sacrifices we hae tae mak.'

The Moor began to steam, a good weather sign, Hector thought. They walked round by the trees with the mist teasing through the wood and, beyond, had a bit of a game trying to break free of what felt like innumerable fences and a paucity of gates. Their lower legs were quickly soaked. However, they soon groped their way up onto the west ridge of the hill, which gave easy going but felt interminable. Just keeping on up had to land them on top and they were all plodding, half asleep, behind Hector, their minds a million miles away – 'in a richt dwam' – so when Hector suddenly stopped, Dave immediately stood on his heels and Specky walked into Dave. But all Hector did was yell at them to 'Look!' When they did they stood fascinated: on the rolling clouds below them a great shadow figure showed, haloed inside the circling bands of a rainbow. Dave let out a brief expletive and Specky took off and wiped his glasses quickly to ensure he wasn't imagining things.

'It's the spectre, isn't it? The Brocken Spectre?'

'Yes,' whispered Hector, as if afraid a raised voice would dispel the image. He waved his arms aloft. The phantom figure did likewise. 'I've only seen one once before. On the Ben. Fantastic.'

'Whit the hell is it?'

'Your shadow just, thrown onto the mist below.'

'But there's jist wan shady an there's three o us.'

'Could be a moral there.' Hector grinned. 'You can only see your own halo.'

Several times the figure came and went, mimicked their movements, grew and shrunk and finally disappeared.

'That was quite something.'

'Very lucky.'

Wide awake now, they pushed on through a chasing sun and shadow world, breathed on with a born-again breeze, exulting in being alive. Over on their left some bird was calling in long, sad, notes.

Suddenly they were at the trig point.

While they stood at the Corbett summit the clouds that had been glued to the hill finally began to move off the Buachaille. From this angle the hill seemed to jag through the clouds like a peak in Skye or some Chamonix aiguille.

'Yon's the Buachaille?'

'Sure is.'

Dave shook his head. 'Ah'm glad you didna suggest going up *it*, then.'

'Oh, there's easy ways up. But this certainly makes it look quite fearsome. I'd no idea.'

Specky grinned, 'From the Rankling La we observed the sublime summit of a very Rum Buachaille.'

Dave put his head back and let out a good screich: 'Yee-ooh!'

'I take it you're happy, then?' Specky grinned.

'Aye. Great. Just great.'

'Worth a couple of pints?'

'Dinna push me too far. Youse two are the tickers. No me.'

'Yet.'

They walked round the rim of the wide summit area, reeling in the view like fishermen with the big one on a line. Hector was good at naming things but even he had to change hill names at times as peaks came in and out of the clouds. No mistaking the Ben, that dome sliced off at the side, their view the mirror-image of those from away up the Great Glen. Mamores and Grey Corries surfed in and out of the waving clouds. Ben Alder's sprawl was clear ('The largest area above 3,500 feet outwith the Cairngorms'), Loch Ericht, Blackwater, Loch Laidon. There was no shortage of big lochs, while the Moor appeared like an extravagantly sequined covering. But it was that wicked thrust of the Buachaille that was remembered most vividly – 'like a skelf in the brain,' as Dave put it.

'So now what?'

They had quite a lengthy 'discussion'. A committee again!

Specky was keen to go down to the Blackwater dam to see the graves of the navvies and Hector would have liked the walk down the birch-fresh glen from there to the village but did not like the extensive area of flat ground in between them and the dam.

'It will be appalling bog.'

'Well, what about going back to the Feithe pass and round and down from there?'

Dave then came in, 'Why don't we just stop f...in aboot an gang back tae the Wey Wey?' – which was what they did, though they angled up from Loch na Feithe to join in on the top of the Devil's Staircase. The Feithe pass was boggy enough that they were glad not to have headed for the dam.

Descending to the pass, they put up the only grouse they saw on the trip, which led to a discussion about the birds' decline. Hector had an unusual speculation (among the more common ones of bad land use, climate changes, and so on) that grouse numbers dropped as the slaughter of predators rose – creating an unnatural balance. 'Balance is all: in nature or human life.'[17]

From the Feithe pass they looked over to the symmetry of the Lairig Gartain, the textbook glaciated, U-shaped valley that separates the sparring partners of the big and wee Buachailles. Hector pointed out how this south-west to north-east line continued in the other direction, up the glen beyond the Blackwater towards Loch Treig.

Their climb from the Feithe pass brought them out to the scoured crest so they missed the Devil's Staircase proper, the line of tight zigzags built by Caulfeild's soldiers, probably in 1750. More than likely the soldiers gave it the familiar name, no doubt with feeling. (Roy's map calls the pass Mam Grinnan.) The mind boggles at the thought of coaches making the ascent.

The trio sat on the bleak top of the pass. ('Aw glaury dubs.') The day continued to improve. There's nothing like Scottish rain to make walkers appreciate Scottish sun. They ate various 'pieces', one of Dave's a roll and butter – and sugar! (His crunching into it set their teeth on edge.) They had an apple each and almost the last of their Harviestoun. Dave lay with his perched precariously on his tight tummy. The other two watched a heavily laden Way Way man approach.

'Hi!' the newcomer greeted. He more or less toppled out of his rucksack.

'His rucker mun hae been aboot eighty litres,' Dave speculated later.

'Bellhaven?' Specky asked. (No Harviestoun for him!)

'Ooh! Oh, yes please. Oh, marvellous.' The man mopped his brow.

'You lot doing the West Highland Way?'

Bit of a rhetorical question. Someone grunted what was taken as a 'yes'.

'My third time,' the man said, a touch of pride in the words.

'Why?' asked the recumbent Dave.

The question obviously took the man by surprise.

'Well, a mate got me to do it two years ago. So I did it again last year. And now this year.'

'Aye, but why?'

'I suppose because I liked it.'

'Next year?'

'Probably.'

Dave nearly voiced his thoughts but you could hardly give a man a beer one moment and call him a fruit and nut case the next. The man thanked them profusely and struggled into his huge pack. Hector and Specky took a hand each and yanked him to his feet.

'Well, must get on. Thanks for the ale. Most kind. Cheerio then.'

And off he went, a rucksack with legs on.

'Do you think his load increases exponentially every year?'

Dave read out the long spiel in their guidebook about the Massacre of Glen Coe in 1692 and they were discussing this when another solitary Way Way man bobbed into view. He mopped his brow and eyed the bottles.

'I'm afraid they're all empty,' Specky apologised.

'Oh, but I never drink,' the newcomer declared. He had been at the Kingshouse the night before. 'Dreadful din from the bar. And, you know, yesterday I met a man, with a dog too, who was walking the West Highland Way the wrong way.'

'The wrong way?'

'What do you mean?'

'He was walking north–south,' and, to make sure the sin was well understood, added, '*From* Fort William.'

The trio weren't quite sure how they were meant to respond to this, so they didn't.

'I mean, everything's wrong. You have to read the guide book backwards, even.'

Dave happened to have their guide in his hand. He opened and read a sentence: ' "Coe Glen through routes easier by superseded long, road military old an is Staircase Devil's The".' He smiled blandly at the man. 'Aye, ah see yir problem, mate.'

'Poor chap,' Specky said after the man had taken himself off, rather hurriedly.

'Is it us?' Dave asked, 'Or here, or whit? We seem tae be attractin Muggles like flees.'

Another figure appeared. In a kilt and a big white beard that would have made a good sporran.

'Let's get the f... oot o here!'

They'd only just started off when they came on a tent by the path. A cheery, red face with a fuzz of ginger beard popped out and asked, 'Like a cuppa?' He waved a battered tin mug.

'Nae thanks. We've just had wir pieces an drinks.'

'Doing the West Highland Way?'

'Aye.'

'Did you get caught in yesterday's rain?'

'Aye, it was a wee bitty wet.'

'Were you on the Way Way?' Specky asked.

The man was only puzzled by the name for a moment. 'No. Yes. I was in Kinloch Leven when it began so I chickened out and spent most of the day in the pub. The Tailrace, next the chip shop, good place', then, to explain his presence, added, 'I meant to be here. For last night. You see, I've a system. Always camp high. Then you get the great views. Dusk and dawn. And going down in the morning means shops are open when you need them, you can have a pint, then up for the splendid solitude again.'

He grinned at them. 'Have a good trip,' he added, and popped back in out of view.

The Way Way crossed a bleak glen with a view down to the dam where all was grim and boggy. Coming to the top of the Devil's Staircase had been a wise choice. (In the Scottish hills any *path* tends to be.) They zigzagged down to cross another bleak glen then flanked along to the penstock where the culvert of water from the dam descends in six massive parallel pipes to Kinlochleven's turbines. Aluminium production is an electrolytic process so requires massive amounts of electricity; thus here, as outside the Fort, the aluminium works made their own electricity. The Fort William scheme actually catches some of its water from the Upper Spey, takes it to Loch Laggan, then Loch Treig, and a tunnel round through the Ben – quite a scheme and dating to 1934. Water from Loch Eilde Mor is fed to the Blackwater by another aqueduct on the other side of the glen, an addition constructed by German prisoners during the First World War. Because of this power supply Kinlochleven had electricity services before Glasgow or London. (The Blackwater dam was built between 1904 and 1907.)

Oddly, Loch Leven was still invisible from this great viewpoint perch, and next day would vanish almost as quickly, so deep set is this fjord of the sea among steep and rugged hills. Garbh Bheinn (*Rough Hill*), along from them, certainly lives up to its name. (When Hector named it a Corbett the others at once hoped he wasn't going to suggest climbing it as well.) The access track wiggled round and down a third corrie, back to the level of enveloping birch, the aluminium works close now.

Two buzzards were circling more or less on their level and they became aware of the birds' odd behaviour – diving and lifting what looked like divots, dropping them and rushing to catch them again in mid-air, a 'game' that only stopped when two noisy hoodies came along, 'for a bit o a stushie' as Dave put it.

The trio descended behind the works to a bridge over the River Leven. Once across, the Way Way heads along Wades Road, which Specky was quick to point out should have an apostrophe and to which Hector added it shouldn't be Wade anyway but Caulfeild. 'I'll show you something. Wait.' When they reached St Paul's episcopal church he indicated a signpost: 'Grey Mare's Waterfall'. 'Notice the spelling of "Grey"?' They turned left and at the main road there was another sign: 'Gray Mare's Waterfall'. 'Notice the spelling, "Gray".'

'The toon canna spell, eh?'

Kinlochleven has the rather sad air of a frontier town that has been passed by. In winter the hills block out the sun and many buildings have red roofs and are painted in cheerful colours to counter the gloom. Until the 1975 local government reorganisation the town was even divided against itself, half Inverness-shire, half Argyll, a police station on each side of the river (for a population never reaching 2,000), and accident or illness seeing ambulances off to Fort William or Oban respectively. ('If you broke a leg on the south side you got your mates to carry you over to a friend's house on the other side before calling out the ambulance.')

Hector did some shopping in the Co-op for their supper while Specky collected their parcel and posted off the Clachgour key. They met up in the Tailrace Inn where its brochure mentioned 'midge screens fitted to all windows'. A London couple doing the Way joined them and they swopped stories. The couple, John and Jean Thomas, had been 'nowhere and back' that day. 'We thought it was going to repeat yesterday when we were hammered on the Devil's Staircase.' They had not done much walking and never anything like an LDP before but were delighted at the experience. 'Southern Uplands Way next,' Jean said. 'Last year we went to Spain and had air traffic controllers striking to maroon us, the hotel was miles from the sea, and the Piccadilly train home broke down. "Never again!" we said. This has been so free and easy. *We* decide everything instead of being at the mercy of others.'

Kinlochleven had brought them to the southern fringe of Lochaber, the last of the three resonant historical provinces threaded by the Way Way: Lennox, Breadalbane, Lochaber. Lochaber's centre is Fort William, another example of how geography and history are interwoven, for it stands at the criss-crossing of lines followed by road, rail and canal and the town's name reiterates the strategic importance. Both Cromwellian and Hanoverian forces controlled this hub encircled by Jacobite clans. The population, at 13,000, is only surpassed by Inverness as a Highland urban sprawl. Nobody would praise Fort William for its civic charms. The town is a bit like a tube of toothpaste that has been stood on by an elephant, splitting and squirting out in every direction under impossible pressure. Fort William was fourteen miles further on by the Caulfeild road, as grand – and different – a day as any along the Way.

Chapter 11

The road and the miles

Wandering along on the north side of Loch Leven they came on another tent, an Ultimate Tramp, perched on a banked table of firm grass, edged by alders over a small burn. A perfect site. Foxgloves and yellow flags flowered beyond. There was just room for another tent. They pitched, rinsed stockings and hung them to dry on the brambles, Hector spread his supplies about, and they lounged outside over a brew while the tent had its airing. Hector looked up and smiled. 'On foreign campsites British parties can always be recognised by their creative mess. I hope the others don't come back soon.'

Of course they did. The dixie of water was just coming to the boil again when the people at the neighbouring tent arrived: a man and a boy, both tanned and whipcord fit by the look of them. If they'd been disgruntled at finding others pitched so near they gave no sign of it.

'Hi!' said the boy, swinging off his pack with an ease that pointed to regular practice. At once he bent to unlace his boots.

'Care for a brew?' Dave asked. 'Waater's bilin.'

Both answered, 'Oh, yes please!', 'That would be nice.'

The boy reached under the flysheet and brought over two mugs. He stood wiggling his toes.

Dave had thrown teabags into the dixie. 'Help yirsels. Milk. Sugar's there. Are youse daein the Wey Wey?'

The boy giggled at the 'Wey Wey' then said, 'No. We do our own routes.'

There wasn't any condescension in the way he said it but the inference was there. The Way Way was for wimps.

The boy poured from the dixie – over the handles – and passed one mug to his father.

'We started at Shiel Bridge a week ago,' the man explained. 'Probably finish at Corrour and train out for fun. No hard and fast route.'

'As long as we climb plenty of Munros.'

'Came over from Nevis youth hostel the day before yesterday ...'

'And did Sgurr a' Mhaim. The Devil's Ridge out and back. Had a fabulous swim in the tarn below Jacob's Ladder.'

'Yesterday we just went off to Fort William for a fester and today we were on the eastern Mamores ...'

'Four Munros. And we watched red-throated divers and saw an eagle really close. I almost jumped on it. Running off the big Binnein. Took a jump off a rock and it was sitting right below. Just gave me a look, spread its wings, and away it went. Magic. It was huge!'

They all found themselves smiling. The kid's enthusiasm was so bubbly fresh and his world so taken for granted.

'We go off nearly every holiday,' the man explained.

'Tessa, that's my sister, and Mummy, they go riding,' the boy added in tones that left no doubt about his opinion of that.

The father smiled, 'We tend to view horses as dangerous at both ends and uncomfortable in the middle.'

'Thanks for the tea. I'm off for a swim. Coming, Dad?'

'Later maybe, Tony.'

They watched the lithe figure pick a way barefoot over the weedy boulders brinking the tide. A static heron unfolded itself, and moved further along the shore. The boy paddled to a big rock and dived into the rippling waters. Beyond, gulls were blowing about like confetti the day after a wedding.

'You've a lively lad there,' Specky said.

'Don't I know it. But catch them young and all that. He actually quite likes riding but only on proper expeditions so we usually end up trekking and Munroing where possible. He's been up about seventy.'

'Mair na me.'

Half-dressed, the boy came over to drape his shirt on the tent. He'd been rubbing himself with it.

'No towel?' Hector asked.

Tony heard. 'Unnecessary weight.' He eyed their set-up. 'Have you got one?'

'One, yes, one. Between us.'

'How many pots and pans? How many stoves?'

'One dixie. One stove.'

'They pass muster then, do they, Dad?'

They all laughed, the man a bit uncertainly.

'We have a pet phrase, Tony,' Hector said: 'You fight every ounce of the way.'

'That's good,' the man nodded.

'Neat,' said the sprog.

'Yesterday we went to see the Grey Mare's Tail when we got back. Do you know it?'

'No.'

'It's just the other side of the town. A fantastic waterfall. Oh, you must go and see it!' said Tony.

'Surprisingly little known,' agreed his father. 'Doesn't show well, being deep in a gorge, but you can stand at the foot so you get the real impression. Yesterday's was quite a show.'

'We got soaked,' the boy said cheerfully. 'I'll take you if you like.'

'After supper then?' Hector suggested, half expecting, half hoping, the boy would forget.

'We could gang tae the pub efter.'

Supper didn't take long. Hector had simply bought a mix of fresh vegetables and when these were ready, ran the veg water into mugs to use with Cup-a-Soups, then added a couple of tins of steak to the vegetables. Young Tony helped them to demolish a melon. The boy reminded them about visiting the waterfall.

Any doubts they had had about this side trip disappeared as they followed a new path past the church and over a rise where they could hear and partly see the great plunge in its hidden recess. They scrambled up the rocky burn to the foot of the falls and stood in the billowing spray. Louis Stott, whose book is the waterfall's equivalent of Munro's *Tables*, says the Grey Mare's Fall is 'one of the best half dozen great falls in Scotland'.

Thomas Pennant in his *Tour in Scotland* (1769) noted the waterfall, and his comments on wandering south on what would become the West Highland Way sounded familiar:

> Left Fort William, and proceeded South along the military
> road on the side of a hill, an aweful height above Loch-Leven
> ... on the left a vast cataract, precipitating itself in a great
> foaming sheet between two lofty perpendicular rocks ... Break-

fast at the little village of Kinloch-Leven on most excellent minced stag, the only form I thought that animal good in. ...

Immediately after leaving Kinloch-Leven the mountains soar..., the sides are covered with wood, the bottoms of the glens filled with torrents that roar amidst the loose stones. After a ride of two miles begin to ascend the black mountain... on a steep road, certainly the highest publick road in Great Britain. On the other side the descent is scarce a mile, but is very rapid down a zig-zag way. Reach the King's house...

Pass near Loch-Talla, a long narrow piece of water, with a small pine wood ... A few weather-beaten pines and birch appear, and in all the bogs great numbers of roots, that evince the forest that covered the country ... Most of this long day's journey from the black mountain was truly melancholy, almost one continued scene of dusky moors, without arable land, trees, houses, or living creatures ...

The Tailrace Inn was crowded with men and women in the garb of walkers, most of whom were noisily 'high', seeing only a day remained of their Way Way. They were bouncing heroic tales of the wet day back and forth. An American voice said, 'Man! I thought you only got rain like that in the tropics.' The decibel level was high. The three grinned their way to the bar and took pints to near the door. There was nothing posh about the place: two rooms had been knocked into one, a fake fire and hideous surrounds installed, the ceiling was low, the floor fake wood, and fruit machine, TV and pool table were all busy. But the 'Walkers Welcome' sticker on the door was reflected in the cheery atmosphere within. 'Eighty miles from Milngavie,' they heard someone yell.

'Eighty Shillings doon the hatch,' Dave muttered.

Hector suddenly said 'Look!' and rose quickly to lead the blind man they'd met at Inveroran to the bar. 'Welcome to bedlam, Ray.'

'Hi. My wife dropped me at the door. What will you have?'

'Na. Na. This is oor roon.'

'Well, thanks, Dave.'

They caught up with each other's doings. The family had crossed Blackmount not long after them and had noted the tent at Blackrock. They stayed comfortably at the Kingshouse.

'That was quite a rough day,' Ray admitted.

'That's one way of putting it.'

The man had quite a store of tales and Dave was astonished at one Ray told which made fun of blindness.

'Why not, Dave? We rag each other about the hills. Being blind doesn't make anyone less human. Rather the opposite.'

Ray's story concerned a couple where the wife had, justifiably, become suspicious about the husband so often being kept late at the office. Sure of her facts, she at last confronted him. 'What would you do if you came in one night and found me in bed with someone else?' To which the husband was not slow in replying, 'I'd shoot his guide dog.'

Another man had been sitting at the outside tables and left the Tailrace Inn at the same time so they walked along together. 'Edwin P. Petzoldt,' he said, in obvious transatlantic tones. They gave their names in return. 'Pleased to meet ya. Gee, it was interesting to hear all about your backpackers' Way. Lock Loman and all that. We got some real big ones back home. Appalachian Trail. John Muir Trail.' Hector and Specky both groaned silently, Dave almost silently. Was everything in America always bigger and better? But Edwin P. Petzoldt proved quite a charmer, asking all about their Way Way doings and background interests – and work. It turned out he was touring Scotland in a mobile home after visiting publishers in London. 'I do sort of Christian books for children,' he explained, 'sort of Peter Rabbit with principles.' He shook their hands at the MacDonald Hotel (he was staying there) and promised Specky he'd look in at the Kirkcaldy Museum and Art Gallery. 'Can't be many Yanks know Peploe. Saw some in Edinboro and I'll do London next week. Say! In Edinboro I went to Edinboro Castle. Real cute. Near died when they fired off some darn cannon, though. Way over the river we could see the Eiffel Tower.' (Startled looks among the trio.[18]) 'Well, nice talking to you folk,' and they all shook hands again.

They lay talking quietly in the gently flapping tent before drifting off to sleep. Sleep was slow in coming partly because of the long light. There had been a perfection of cloudlessness to end the day, a sunset of subdued reds, the afterglow circling the whole sky and hurrying back for dawn.

They were not early up next day. Hector forgot to set the alarm and nature took advantage of the lapse. The voices of Tony and his father roused them. They crawled out to a day which was obviously going to be a hot one.

'Of course, now we're nearly done. Morning, Tony.'

'Morning.'

'Morning all.'

'By God, one of you doesn't half snore.'

'Sorry, it's me. Hopeless. Hector disna notice and *he* taks a sleepin pill.'

'Self-defence,' Specky added. 'Never used them before.'

'You snore too, dad.'

'Thanks, son.'

A slight element of competitiveness might have been discerned. Nobody needed to voice the thought, 'We can't be shown up by them.' Breakfasts were treated seriously and efficiently.

Tony and his father departed for the Devil's Staircase and the BFs set off on their last lap, both groups walking together for a bit in companionable silence.

The jealous barrier of the Mamores is largely sidestepped by the track of the Lairig Mor (*the big pass*) which sidles along below the southern slopes of the range to approach Fort William. The West Highland Way, however, cuts through to Glen Nevis some miles short of the town, as if to tempt one to finish on Ben Nevis. The start of the day gives a steep pull up of about 250 metres but legs that have come this far will not complain too much and plenty of pauses should be made to look back, down, for an ever-receding view of character. Loch Leven takes on its true fjord-like appearance, and the colourful roofs of the town are seen through shivery birchwoods with the hills beyond looming over darkly. West, the watery way leads the eye to the cone of the Pap of Glencoe, a shape as familiar here as it is from the Ballachulish bridge. Only, on foot, there's more time to look and admire.

The trio were in two minds as to their ascent: up the wee tarred road or on to the filling station for the official path? In order not to argue in front of their neighbours Dave and Specky left Hector to decide and he went for path, not tarmac. They said goodbye to their fellow campers there. Just before the Mamore Lodge road, however, there was a made footpath which merged with the Kinlochleven one higher up and gave a useful shortcut. They took the climb slow and easy. Specky took plenty of photos.

'You'll hae tae show them at the club.'

'What! With you two heckling?'

'Absolutely!'

Specky never did do a slide show. Unbeknown to him, from the start there had been a fault with the shutter and every picture he had taken was ruined. He was mortified.

The toil up was sweaty work and, sun or not, their passing called up some midges. But a swat and curse from Specky indicated they had met the third plague of the Highlands in summer.

'Hey! That was a horsefly,' the victim said.

'Cleg,' countered Dave.

'The Scots would have a word for it,' Specky laughed. 'Cleg. Cleg.' He repeated the word with the concentration of a wine-taster. 'It suits.'

'Aye, an aw they tourist brochures dinna mention them either. Midges, ticks, clegs. Nae wonner the Heilanders cleared oot.'

They were soon back on the Caulfeild line up from the head of Loch Leven, perhaps the best part of the day, the going excellent, the views magnificent. ' "And the sun shines and the road shines, / And the wine's in the cup",' Specky quoted.

This Caulfeild's track is now overlaid by the Lairig Mor estate road from Mamore Lodge but must, in its preservation and improvement, give a good idea of what the military road was like in its prime. They crossed the first of the Mamore streams, the birches standing quiet. Hector put up his umbrella. The sun was wicked.

A bronchial redstart perched on a stone but, as they watched, seemed to dive into the heather as a large bird rushed past.

'Whit the hell?'

'Sparrowhawk.'

'Weel, he missed.'

A woodpecker drummed down in the woods as if to call them back to work. Not for the first time Hector's brolly nearly caught Specky in the eye. They were too similar in height. Specky strode on, too hot to comment. Dave lingered to take in the view back down, for the last time. The consciousness of ending was suddenly sad. They were on the last day. The path twists and turns as it rises, then the long open pass lay ahead. Back behind them, they could see dots of figures following and, over on the Devil's Staircase side, the parallel pipes of the hydro works.

Another bird flitted across the track, instantly recognised by its white rump pattern. 'Wheatear,' said Hector.

'White erse,' said Dave. 'That's whit it wis till a hunner year ago when the guid auld wird wis thocht tae be rude. But it's whit it is. Wheatear is bloody nonsense.'

Sheep stood to watch them pass, either being casual about the regular stream of walkers or rendered immobile by the day's heat. They'd seen few deer throughout their walk (more roe than red deer) but that was simply because deer drift high in summer for coolness and to avoid flies and midges. 'The sun's keeping the little devils away,' Specky grinned. The road stretched away for visible miles. Hector likened it to a knotless string and said he preferred a more fankled challenge. There were dots of another party far ahead too. Their feet grew stinging hot with the hard surface.

They came on a middle-aged man sitting beside one big burn, his boots beside him. By the state of his shirt and shorts he'd just finished sitting *in* the burn. He grinned a bit sheepishly out of a face the colour of supermarket meat and they collapsed beside him.

'I just jumped in as I was.'

'Just glad you left some water for us.'

'I'm Mike Taylor, from Preston.'

They variously gave their names.

'Kinda hot, eh?'

'Ooh aye, kinda drouthy.'

Hector took the sweat rag from the small of his back and actually wrung it out. Mike grimaced. Specky said, 'That's revolting.'

'Better than "nappy rash" from the sweat getting between the cheeks,' Hector retorted.

Dave was quite disappointed: despite the fierce strangulation of his T-shirt, no sweat ran out. Garments were thrown aside. They began unlacing boots.

Taking boots off was always a treat. Dave tossed his 'bauchles' aside with a sigh of relief, Hector perched his to air on top of a granite boulder, Specky was left hopping about on one foot.

'Whit are you lowpin aboot fir? Hae you stood on a jaggie?'

'I can't get the bloody boot off.'

'What do you mean?'

'Just what I said. My foot's stuck inside.'

Specky sat and struggled with the recalcitrant boot. The laces were loose. There seemed no reason why it shouldn't come off.

'Help, you buggers.'

Dave obliged. The boot remained on Specky's foot.

'You having us on?'

Specky shook his head. 'Hold it still,' he ordered and, while Dave did so, he pulled with all his strength. Suddenly he flew over backwards. His foot had come out, out of stocking as well as boot. He muttered something about his toes but the others were staring, then giggling, at the boot with the stocking flopping out of it. Hector took hold of the stocking and yanked. The stocking remained stuck. All three, in mounting frustration, tried and failed to pull the stocking from Specky's boot. (Mike Taylor's face was a study.) Something held firm at the toe. Eventually Specky succeeded but only after curling his feet to hold the boot down and heaving with all his might. For a second time he went flying backwards.

Dave was inspecting the boot. Peering. Prying.

'Gie's yir stockin.'

The toe was inspected then a big grin crossed Dave's face.

'You'll no believe it.'

'Try me.'

'You ken they black slugs?'

'So?'

'There must hae been wan in yir bit when you pit it on. You squashed it wi yir taes. An it stuck yir stockin.'

Specky, then Hector, both inspected boot and stocking and had to agree with Dave's diagnosis. Even the man Mike had a look.

Hector said, 'Someone should do some research. We could be on to something. A natural superglue.'

'Very funny.'

'No. Seriously. Who'd believe what we've just seen? All that grip from a wee slug.'

'Big slug,' Specky corrected. 'You never see wee ones.'

As far as is known the research has not yet been undertaken.

They did things with that burn. An otter couldn't have been more thorough or original. Mike struggled out of his nearly dry clothes to jump in again.

'That's the longest I've ever been in a pool,' Hector said as he scrambled out onto the bank and put up his sunshade. '*Parasol* a change from *parapluie*, eh?'

'Walkers coming,' Specky observed.

'Looks like John and Jean.'

There was a scurry to gain some respectability and they were sitting looking like schoolboys caught in an orchard when the Thomases halted.

'Hi!'

'Hi!'

'John and Jean,' said Hector, 'Mike.'

'Hi.'

'Mind if we join you? Could do with a paddle.'

Once they'd paddled, Jean asked a question that got stares rather than any spoken reply: 'Anyone thirsty?'

John pulled out a can of peaches, a big can of peaches (822 grams, the label said). They all looked at each other.

'There was a dent in the can so it was reduced.'

The Jiffy opener seemed to take for ever.

There wasn't much finesse in their demolition job. Fingers reached in and grappled slithery segments, cramming them into their mouths.

'If ah wis a cat, ah'd purr.'

'Amen to that.'

Specky then burrowed into his rucksack.

'I'd forgotten this. Sort of worked to the bottom. I've carried it all the way from Tyndrum.'

He held up a chunk of shapeless fruit cake and in turn poured crumbly portions into cupped hands.

'Must be Betty's,' he apologised.

'Wonder how ma wee speug's daein?' Dave muttered to himself but Specky heard and struggled to keep a straight face. Sparrow was the last thing he would have called Betty.

Hector brought them back to reality.

'We're not out of this oven yet. Let's get on.'

With some reluctance they prepared for the road again, all except Mike, though he put on his now dry clothes to avoid burning any further.

'I'm going to snug in the shadow by the bridge there and sleep. Far too hot for walking. I'll move on later. Or tomorrow. Can't stand heat like this.'

His pack looked fairly small.

'Got a tent?'

'No; just a light sleeping bag and a bivvy bag. Quite adequate for the circumstances.'

'Food? Stove?'

'No stove. Saves weight. Plenty rations, though. Oatcakes, cheese, tin of sardines, chocolate. I'll be fine.'

They all said goodbye and turned to the hard, stony slog of the track. 'Walk softly,' Hector muttered to himself. 'Like a butterfly on tiptoes.' Jean said, 'At least it's downhill soon.'

The trio laughed and Hector commented, 'I've heard that a few times since Milngavie.'

The track went steadily *up* for another half hour. Tigh-na-Sleubhaich, once a Mamore keeper's house, lay just over the gentle watershed, roofless but with a strange symmetry of triple gables and chimneys, a lone tree behind and decayed machinery like sculptures on the grass. The road on seemed to snake away for miles. Well, it did. They drank from the burn.

'Is that safe?' Jean asked.

'Never harmed me yet,' Hector replied. 'A pal of mine once was told off during a course in the Cairngorms. Didn't he know about sheep's liver flukes, what old shepherds died of? His reply was "If it's *old* shepherds die of it, that's OK by young me" – and carried on drinking.'

Looking back from the watershed (around 330 metres) they could see at least five different individuals or groups coming up the track.

'You know,' Specky said, 'doing it "the wrong way" would have one great advantage. You'd have the going to yourself.'

'Hoo dae ya mean?'

'Most walkers will have left Kinlochleven between nine and ten so there's a surge, like this, then nobody. Stop and you'll be caught up. Everyone's passing and being passed, just like we've been. But going the other way you'll have one busy spell and then nobody.'

'Interesting theory.'

The building, Lairigmor, once a Callert shepherd's home, was a tumble of stones. How often they'd seen the sad signs of vanished life. No wonder Scottish descendants are found in every corner of the world. Specky reckoned this century's diaspora, with two world wars, was one reason the 'Great' had gone out of Britain. 'Too long a haemorrhage.'

A good path broke off at Lairigmor to cross a col west of Mam na Gualainn to Callert on Loch Leven, a one-time ferry over to Invercoe for man and beast. Drovers often swam their charges over narrows like Loch Leven. They really did not like the military roads, which were too hard on the beasts' feet.

Mullach nan Coirean, the last Munro of the Mamore extravagance of eleven Munros,[19] thrust out a hammerhead spur, Meall a' Chaorainn (*rowan hill*), which their route would circle, a strange, red plateau world quite unlike anything on the switchback of spiky peaks eastwards. Crags, screes and the gashes of racing streams fell to the glen. The ancient sites of summer shielings could be picked out. Here the crofters of Blarmachfoldach (four or five miles on) sent the cattle for the few summer weeks when higher pastures had sweet grass, usually in charge of the women and children. A few crofts still survive but the shieling system, like *bergeries* in Corsica, has gone for ever. All too soon the track reached the start of the plantations that would be their lot to the end. They paused at a sheep fank for another drink of water. Later Specky estimated they each drank about ten pints of liquid that day and nobody had to go out for a pee in the night. The almost desert heat of the pass, far from easing, grew stuffy and hotter, 'as if the very trees were sweating'.

A mile and a bitty on they came out of trees to look down on the small road which had climbed up and along from Fort William and here swung over to the isolated farm of Lundavra which stood above a lochan with a circling quarrel of gulls and a few guardian pines and a pass through to Glen Righ and the Corran Ferry. Here they paused briefly, for John and Jean were planning to follow the road (still the old military road) all the way to the Fort. They had a sleeper booked that night.

A bumble bee was noisily working along the selfheal below the orchid-covered bank, 'fumbling the flowers', as Specky quoted. (Did the man never stop?) Dave watched and then said, 'Ye ken, a bumble bee is aerodynamically impossible. That bulk wi that wing span shouldna work.' Hector removed some spikey bits of whin from between boot and stocking then swung his rucker on. They took the hint. They could see the couple striding along, tiny figures on a long grey switchback of road, fuzzy with heat shimmer.

'Don't envy them five miles of tarmac.'

Dave looked at the official Way ahead.

'An ah dinna really care fir five miles of f...in spruce.'

The route now follows an artificial line created for the West Highland Way, a 4-kilometre stretch screwed into hills towards Glen Nevis, mostly making a way through spruce plantations. The path is well made, bridges cross burns and high stiles cope with forest fences. Ben Nevis reared its bulk ahead, 'like a hippo surfacing', Hector suggested.

The section along under Sgorr Chalum offers something of an athletic switchback, plunging down (wooden steps even) to bridge a wee rocky gorge (the usual birch cladding) and then puts in some uphill contortions.

They had almost given up on visiting Dun Deardail when they came on a made path to the prehistoric dun (*fort*). This is a vitrified fort, a type where the stonework has been fired, with such an intense heat generated that the rocks have melted – whether this was done intentionally or not is uncertain and how such high temperatures were produced is a mystery.

'Could they archaeologists no build wan and set it on fire an see?'

The stony descent to Glen Nevis soon picked up a major forest track, rather tame, with easy-angled walking, some of the slopes felled, and the backside of the Ben across the valley hardly an attractive view. A bit of an anticlimax. They'd seen nobody since the big pass but now a figure appeared ahead. Despite using a pair of poles, he was limping badly. They soon caught up.

'Hi.'

'Oh, hello.'

The man wiped his brow.

'You in trouble?' Hector asked, eyeing the bulge of muddy bandage linking boot and shin.

'No. Well, yes, but no more than usual. I went over on my ankle near the Kingshouse. Quite painful actually. Swelled up so getting my boot off – or back on – was going to be a problem so I just left it on and added more strapping to stiffen the ankle. Stood in a burn for ages too. I'll have it seen to at Fort William; maybe.'

'You mean you've just kept the boot on ever since the Kingshouse? Overnight?'

'The landlady at the B&B was most understanding.'

Hector shook his head. 'You really should get it X-rayed, just in case.'

'Oh yes. But I'll finish the Way first.'

They wished the man well and went on.

'Bloody hell. Whit some folks dae!'

'Good on him,' Specky said.

Hector commented, 'He probably did the right thing. If he'd taken the boot off he'd certainly not have got it back on, and the ankle is being supported. But it must be agony.'

'Wonder how he did it?'

'Doesn't take much. I once sprained an ankle on a wee pothole in a tarred road. Took longer to clear up than if I'd broken it.'

'Wonder what the fallout rate is for the Way Way? There's a hell of a lot of innocents doing it.'

'Weel, ye hae tae stairt some wey!' Dave said, a bit defensively. 'Ah've learned a lot, ye ken.'

'We're not finished yet. Don't tempt fate.'

A few minutes later Dave said, 'Take a keek. We're being followed. An no by Hopalong.'

Not many people caught up on the Fifers but this person did, and rapidly, though he carried a substantial rucksack with a rolled Therm-a-Rest under the flap on top. He looked leathery-browned, lean and fit. Almost sheepishly Dave asked him if he was doing the Way.

There was hesitation before 'yes', so he was more or less forced to confess: 'I'm also doing Land's End to John o'Groats.'

'Lucky you.'

'That's why yir goin like the clappers.'

The man smiled. 'Yes. And the shame is the fitness will soon disappear after the finish.'

Hector laughed. 'At least you're using your fitness. Doing coast-to-coast you're just getting into a state of grace when you stop.'

Hector and Strider (as Specky called him) walked on, talking away together, while the other two followed.

'If we dinna watch oot, Hector'll be awa fir John o'Groats.'

'No way.'

'I'm jist jokin.'

'He's quite a bloke, Hector. I bet he's a superb doctor too.'

'Aye. A quiet one but they're often the real toughies.'

The two in front eventually paused and the man (they never learned his name) gave a cheery 'goodbye' to Dave and Specky and went on, accelerating with disgusting ease.

'Glide, don't stride,' Specky smirked.

Hector said, 'He's going to pull up to camp by Lochan Meall an t-Suidhe tonight. He'll have the top of the Ben to himself in the morning.'

'Might be above midge level too.'

'He was telling me about a chap, Norman Croucher, who recently did a Groats End walk, with *two* artificial legs, from above the knee, and it was his second time.'

'I've heard him lecture,' Specky said. 'He'd been up Cho Oyu. There was a lovely moment during questions when a female, all cooing and "dear boying", asked how he had lost his legs and he replied, "As a youngster I got drunk and collapsed on a railway line. Train did it."'

They turned off back along a lower forestry track as markers directed, then walked down from the forestry houses to reach the Glen Nevis Restaurant and Bar next to the campsite. 'Ah!' said Dave but then they paused, a bit irresolute. The midges might be bad on such a warm, muggy evening, the mugginess possibly a prelude to rain again.

'Let's try the hostel.'

'No harm.'

So they walked along to the familiar old timber building. Didn't appear over-busy. They went into the lobby: Hector, Dave, Specky. In any other order the result might have been different. Hector neared the reception desk and then suddenly wheeled round and walked out again, the other two dutifully following and only outside did they variously question Hector's odd behaviour.

'Whit the f...?'

'What was that about?'

Hector looked from one to the other. 'Him.'

'Him?'

'Bill Payne.'

'F...!' 'No!'

'He was taking his boots off. So what do we do?'

'Payne or rain?' Specky offered.

As one, two voices answered, 'Rain!'

So they walked back down the glen road for the campsite. There seemed to be a mile of trim beech hedge before the entrance drive. 'Looks awful posh,' Dave commented as they walked up to the admin block and shops. The 30-acre setting was very park-like, with everything tidy, plenty of trees and privacy, a clutter of 'motor homes' filling one area (remember when they were simply 'camping cars'?) and a colourful collection of tents where they eventually came to roost. Most of them seemed to be Way Way walkers, a good proportion from abroad.

They pitched in the allotted spot and went off to have showers. ('We've paid for them, after all.') The style and standard of the facilities were exceptional by campsite standards. There seemed to be a lot of people just standing about in the block. Lots of talk but, when they went out, one by one after showering, they found why. The midges were back on the warpath.

The midges were maneaters, piranhas, and a whole campsite of sweaty flesh was like giving a cow pie to Desperate Dan. 'Hey, you know you can have a midge density of a couple of million on an area the size of a football pitch.' (About a tenth of the area of the camping site.) They did not thank Specky for this statistic. Sealed inside the tent, coil burning, they were 'perspiring freely' and gagging for oxygen. A wail came from the tent next door.

'What can I do? What can I do? They're driving me mad.'

Dave yelled, 'Oi, matey, jist open the door an let the buggers oot.'

'Are there any recorded suicides because of midges, Specky?'

'Could well be. But I'll tell you this. In the seventeenth or eighteenth century a minister was forced on the people round Loch Maree. They were so incensed that they took the minister and stripped him naked, tied him to a tree and left him to the midges.'

'And?'

'He took the hint and left.'

They decided they could skip a visit to a pub, even the one next door.

'Not a pint to die for.'

Dave, however, had promised to give Betty a ring. 'She who must be obeyed.' As he crawled out he added, 'I may be gone some time.'

'So who's doing the quotes now?'

There was a silence. Specky got out his book. Hector then said, 'Quite a lad, our Dave.'

'Despite his adjectives?' Specky teased.

'Actually, they're mostly adverbs. No, he's a wee toughie. What's so funny?'

Specky just shook his head.

'He's been taking everything in like a sponge. Hugging life. That's good.'

'Here he comes,' Specky said.

Dave was in tearing spirits.

'She's expectin!'

They both offered their congratulations.

'Ah phoned fir a taxi tae.'

'What?'

'Is it expected that soon?'

'We've Ben Nevis to climb.'

Dave bawled at them to shut up. He could hardly speak for laughing.

'Ah'm no goin hame. It's just for tae tak us tae the Fort. This caws fir a celebration.'

They celebrated, an all too frequent prologue to ascents of Ben Nevis, and it was largely Dave's wanting to return to Fife quickly that had them setting off at all next morning for the summit of Scotland. Sunset was all warning smoke with no fire.

Chapter 12

On top of the world

If Dave hadn't been in such a state they might have left the Ben for another day – or even another visit – but then the ascent was also very much the climax of the Way Way as planned. Dave was keen to go regardless of the 'fairly manky conditions', as Specky called them.

'We'll go up the Tourist Path,' Hector sighed. 'If it improves we could go down and round the Arête[20] or something.'

'An if it gets worse?'

'We come down the same way,' and Hector made a wry face. The Tourist Path was the last choice of route for someone who climbed.

'Bugger it! Ah'm sorry.'

'Nothing to be sorry about. I climbed the Ben seven times before I ever had a view. And you could wait *weeks* for a good day.'

'So much for the books that tell you to sit still if caught in mist. Do that on the Ben and you could be a fossil before anyone found you.'

They set off on a gurly morning, early all the same, up to cross by the bridge at the hostel. They stood on it for a while, as so many do. A dipper flew up the river, the familiar ticking voice coming from under their feet. In Gaelic the bird is the *smith of the stream*.

'Extraordinary,' Hector commented. 'It too was persecuted last century as vermin. Could have been wiped out like the osprey.'

A wagtail was working along the pebbles edging the river, followed, and pestered by, an importuning young one. They were still standing on the bridge when Hector touched their arms in turn and made signs to be quiet, and look. Working along the riverside path was a fox. In that light the beast appeared huge. Very dog-like, except for the extravagant brush, behaving dog-like too, sniffing every tree bole, clump of rushes or boulder, then squatting to leave its mark. 'Vixen,' Specky breathed. She passed the end of the bridge and moved on upstream out of sight. 'It's always *movement* that betrays. Lucky we saw her first.' They were moving off the bridge when a heron, possibly put up by the vixen, came beating down the river, took one look at them, and flapped up and over the trees.

They followed the path up the first, steep, 150 metres to reach the main 'tourist track', which had been built originally as a pony track servicing a summit observatory. This track came up from Achintee on the north bank at a gentler angle and rose steadily below the crags and gullies of Meall an t-Suidhe (711 metres), a low western outlier of the Ben, to work round onto the col leading to the toilsome upper slopes of Britain's highest summit. On the col is a lochan often called 'the halfway lochan'. (It's 567 metres.)

They'd hardly reached the pony track when a gang of youths barged past, slithering and sliding, hopping on the verges, giving no greeting, looking puffy of face and puffing of lungs. ' "Slow and easy goes far in the day," ' Specky quoted to Hector who was beside him. 'So said Moleskin Joe, in one of Patrick MacGill's books, him that wrote *Children of the Dead End* about the building of the Blackwater dam.'

'I've read it,' Hector said. 'There's a recent reprint out. Great stories. Every time I go on Rannoch Moor now I half expect to find a skeleton of one of the navvies.'

'I always hope to find the remains of a well-to-do Victorian gentleman.'
'Why?'

'He might have had a pocket full of sovereigns. Think what they'd be worth now.'

'What does?' Dave asked, having only heard the last words.

Specky recapped, then Hector produced a statistic. 'You know, there's over sixty folk have gone off in the Scottish hills this century and never been found.'

'That's a lot.'

'Wan or twa maybe murders?' suggested Dave.

'Maybe.'

'Sixty.'

'Think too how people wander round, lost for days. There was a case years ago in Snowdonia when kids got caught in mist and pitched tents to wait for it to clear. For several days hundreds of people were scouring the Carnedds looking for them yet, if they'd followed the burn down just a couple of miles, they'd have come on a farm.'

There are imposing views up Glen Nevis to the Mamore peaks, dominated by Sgurr a' Mhaim and Stob Ban. Well, usually; they were cloud-capped now. The trio kept up a steady pace, passing and being passed. Most people were sensibly dressed but there was one man in scanty clothing and sandals: 'An accident waiting to happen'.

Out of interest Specky was listening to voices and noting nationalities. By the end of the day he'd got Japanese, Australian, French, German, Irish, Italian, South African, American, Dutch and some Eastern European countries.

The path, even with much maintenance work, was rough (gritty granite) and bouldery. Eventually they swung up and round by the Red Burn hollow to reach Lochan Meall an t-Suidhe (try Meowl an tee – *hill of the seat*), where they walked over to sit on some boulders above the grey waters. Rings breaking on the surface pointed to trout in the lochan. The cloud level was teasing along, just above – their halfway point. A path runs along through the pass and leads round to the great north-east cliffs of the Ben, 'the grandest array of cliffs on any Scottish mountain'. Sadly, this array of cliffs is hidden away so is only seen by the more adventurous.

'I reckon only one in a hundred coming up the Tourist Route has any idea of what the other side's like.'

'They can look down from the top.'

'That's assuming you can see anything.'

'Actually all the guides and things mention the danger of cliffs, especially in mist – or in winter when there are huge cornices.'

'But how many of these punters read anything? Even the notice boards at the start?'

'To be safe, a lot keep well left coming down to avoid the cliffs and instead end up in Five Finger Gully, the big catchment of gullies on the Glen Nevis side. Nearly as many die there as come to grief on the cliffs.'

The temperature had already dropped and the trio put on their waterproof jackets and nibbled their chosen goodies. The sandwiches they'd bought in the pub the night before were kept for the summit. Coming along the loch path, from the Allt a' Mhuilinn side, was a man, middle-aged and walking with arm crutches. When he reached them, he paused to say hello, and they noticed he had two artificial feet. The man had stopped for just one reason. He'd been staying at the CIC hut[21] and was desperate to know how Liverpool had got on in their midweek match with Manchester United. He'd asked the wrong people.

Some Italians came along from the Tourist Path, and were put back on course again. They were from Milan, on a bus tour of 'bonnie Scotland' and were well wrapped up though not in real outdoor gear.

'What a shame the Ben's always like this,' Hector sighed.

They wended up the zigzags in silence.

While the angle eases off thereafter the ground is nothing but a great stony waste, here and there with patches of dirty snow, and the cliff edge marked by the upwelling of weary clouds. A few starry saxifrages simply looked pathetic – and were certainly the highest flowers in the country. One of the black stones suddenly seemed to explode upwards, giving them a fright till it proved to be a raven, which went off, mocking, into the murk.

'This is my least favourite bit of the Ben,' Hector said. 'And it's so often like this.' He waved his hand at the blowing mist. Ghost-like figures came and went. The noisy gang of youths they'd met at the start came past again, silent and looking much less cocky.

'Where have they been?'

'Probably shot off through by the loch, or tried a shortcut and went astray in the mist.'

' "A stone's throw out on either hand / From that well-ordered road we tread / And all the world is wild and strange," ' Specky said and, before anyone could ask, added 'Kipling'.

'Ony poetry aboot the Ben, then?' Dave asked.

'Surprisingly little and, like Ben Lomond, most of it pretty poor, even if by people like Wordsworth or Keats.'

'Keats. What did he write about?'

'Ben Nevis. Not a very good poem. But he climbed the Ben. I've a theory the hill killed him.' They looked at Specky, so he continued, 'He set off from Lancaster, aged twenty-two, with a friend, Charles Brown, walked through the Lake District, climbing Helvellyn and Skiddaw, before heading into Scotland for the Burns country. They walked fifteen miles up Loch Lomondside then Glen Croe, thinking the Rest and Be Thankful was an inn where they could find breakfast. They went on by Inveraray and Loch Awe to Oban and across Mull. Keats was ill there but still came on to do the Ben – in awful conditions – but by Inverness was ordered home by a doctor. They sailed from Cromarty. After all that rough tramping his health was never the same. He was only twenty-five when he died. So I reckon the Ben "did for him".'[22]

They were silent a minute, then Dave said, 'An I always thocht Keats was a richt peely wally Jessie.'

The observatory is perhaps the Ben's most interesting human story. Specky knew all about it, as they expected. 'Thomas Stevenson (of lighthouse fame and the father of RLS) first suggested high-level weather observations but government funds were not available. In 1880 and 1881 Clement E. Wragge (nicknamed Inclement Rag) climbed the hill daily, June to October, to take readings. The observatory had to be built with money raised by public appeals, and a pony track constructed to the top. It took one season to build and was in use for twenty-one years. An estimated 4,000 visitors called in the year after it opened (1884), and later a basic hotel was built for visitors.

'There was a toll on the track up from Achintee. Lightning once started a fire in the kitchen, and winds could be strong enough to stop all observations outside. (There is a delightful picture in a book of playing ping-pong on an ice-carved table.) A weekly contact with Fort William in winter was all they could manage – unless climbers called. Rubbish was simply tipped down the nearest gully, which climbers soon named Gardyloo gully (the bucket-emptier sometimes had to be belayed for this job). Some of Scott's polar team trained on the Ben and the *Scotia* expedition was led by one of the staff. A summer volunteer went on to win a physics Nobel Prize and in his speech pointed to the original stimulus coming from his stay on Nevis. On the verge of air travel and other vital scientific advances, the observatory shut down owing to government cutbacks in 1904.'

An English vicar as early as 1789 noted there were thirty cairns on Nevis and various names and initials in bottles and so on. Another book tells of a band of army officers out all day from five in the morning who came back beaten by bogs and perpendicular rocks, thankful for a break in the clouds: 'if those vapours had continued, there would have been no means left for them to find their way down, and they must have perished with cold, wet, and hunger'.

The Naylor brothers in 1871 (on a Groats End walk) referred to Nevis as 'the Ben', which Hector had always thought a modern familiarity. They failed because their guide became ill. This gentleman was 'mortified to have failed, for he had been up the hill 1,200 times'.

When the trio reached the summit, in about three and a half hours, they could see very little. The remains of the observatory were topped by a wee tin shelter.[23] ('Up there to be above winter snow.') There were now a hundred cairns, memorials, trig point, view indicator. Dirty patches of snow lay on top of the wet, black rocks. Dave suggested a couple of hours with a JCB would improve things.

Maybe it was as well people didn't know the sort of statistics that had been gleaned from the observatory over the period 1883–1904. There were 261 gales a year (i.e. winds above 50 mph, gusts sometimes three times greater), the average mean temperature was just below freezing, the summit was only clear on about fifty days a year and the average rainfall was 157 inches. If the Ben had been a bit higher it would have grown a glacier.

Dave asked a man to take a photo of them all and he turned his rucksack at his feet to ensure the mascot was in full view. The teddy was a bit the worse for wear, never having been removed from its perch, not infrequently soaked, sat on and having close encounters with peat or granite.

'But at least she'll hae proof.'

'So, now? You could throw the thing over the cliff,' Specky suggested.

Dave just shook his head. Grinned. 'Way Way goes home.'

'Way Way?'

'That's her name. She earned it. An dinna you grin like yon. You'll hae yir wings clipped when ye'r marrit.'

Sitting on one of the cairns was the man with crutches. He grinned at them. 'Liverpool won!'

'F...in hell!' Dave said, once out of hearing. 'That seems tae be mair tae him than getting up the Ben.'

'No sign o yon mannie we met yesterday? Strider.'

'Och, he'll be over the Arête and halfway to Spean Bridge by now. He's meeting his wife for a blowout meal at The Old Pines near the Commando Memorial, then he'll camp by Loch Lochy, cross the Munros and Ben Tee to Loch Lochy youth hostel before heading for the west.' Hector sighed, 'Enviable fitness.'

'Maybe we should turn round and head for Milngavie. Not waste our fitness.'

The clouds were flying at half mast so below the level of the screes they were able to remove waterproofs. They swung round onto the Glen Nevis slopes. Past the top zigzag the sun came out.

'Wid you credit that?'

'Typical.'

They sat in the sun, peeled off sweaty shirts to dry and simply enjoyed sitting, doing nothing, though the moments were tinged with the knowledge of endings. Sgurr a' Mhaim was doing a good imitation of a volcano, the clouds streaming off its conical grey bulk.

'Ah'm stairvin,' sounded like a suggestion that they should move. Dave reached for his Raith Rovers T-shirt.

'Hold on a minute, Dave. There's something on your back.' Specky inspected the small of Dave's back. 'Yuch, it's a tick.'

'Shit! Can you pu the bugger aff?'

Hector quickly said, 'Don't pull it! You'll just leave the head behind and it can turn nasty.'

'Oh, thanks.'

'So what do I do?'

Hector grinned, 'I'm told a lighted cigarette held to a tick makes it let go.'

'But no one smokes,' Specky began, then saw Hector's grin.

'What about a lighter then?' he grinned back.

'You're no pittin a f…in lighter on me!'

'Hey, I thought all blacksmiths were incombustible.'

'Stop takin the piss an dae summit.'

'OK. Move over, Specky. Bend, Dave.'

Hector peered down, took hold of the tick – and instantly, there was a yelp from Dave. Hector opened his hand to show the bloated, purply, pea-sized body, its legs scrabbling feebly. Not the most endearing of creatures.

'Want to squash it?' Hector asked Dave. 'It's full of your blood.'

Dave looked at Hector, too aghast for speech. He could no more have handled the tick than he could have eaten it. Hector just shrugged and dumped it on the ground, took a sharp chuckie and dispatched the bloodsucker. It popped satisfactorily. Dave wrinkled his nose.

'How did you get it out so easily?' Specky asked.

'You get a good grip, right down on the front parts, then give a sharp wrench, anti-clockwise.'

'Anti-clockwise – why?'

'Obvious – they burrow in clockwise.'

They both looked but Hector wasn't smiling.

Back at the campsite they brewed and lazed beside the tents, sat at the picnic tables writing postcards, read a bit, had showers, brewed some more and generally acted the tourist with great contentment, but there was to be one last 'experience' to be added before they headed home.

Doctor Hector (sod's law) had gone along to the youth hostel (risking Bill Payne) to buy a new handbook, so just Dave and Specky were standing outside the tent, enjoying an evening free of midges, when there was a loud whoosh that turned their eyes on a nearby tent. As they turned there was a blast and a figure shot out of the tent door followed by a blossoming of flames. The figure scrabbled to his feet yelling 'Bill! Maggie!' and tried to get back into the tent. But it was too hot, the fire too fierce and he just stood screaming. Two figures, however, burst out, fabric flaming and bubbling on their shoulders, hair smouldering, dazed, horrified.

Dave, perhaps more used to the horrors of fire, was the first of the campers to react. He yelled, 'Specky! Get on the phone for an ambulance!' while he grabbed one of the pair (the girl Maggie, it proved) and poured the contents of their water carrier over her. ('F...ing baptised her,' he reported later.) The one who had been blasted out of the tent did something similar with his mate Bill, until he saw Bill's face and, at the sight, he half keeled over, spewing out his supper.

The one unplanned amusing incident went almost unnoticed. There was a big tent near and the family's mum had placed bacon and butter in a bucket of water to keep them fresh. The father grabbed the bucket and threw the water over the flaming tent. This had little effect on the flames but produced a most unusual fry-up.

There was nothing at all amusing about those who'd been caught in the tent. The one who had largely escaped was shaking and sobbing, obviously in shock. He'd had a second's warning of what was happening and dived for the door, his exit speeded up by a 'kick' as the Gaz cylinder exploded.

The bloke Bill was in a right mess. He'd been changing cylinders on one stove while another stove was burning under a dixie of soup – and he fumbled and dropped the newly pierced cylinder. This spun and danced as if jet-propelled (which is roughly what it was) and liquid Gaz shot up over Bill and the tent. With a naked flame a foot away the inevitable was almost instant. Bang! Bill had his face running down onto his chest. His girl's hands and face were burnt by flaming plastic as she clawed her way out, dragging the temporarily blinded Bill after her. The whole incident just took seconds.

Dave was kneeling by Maggie, giving occasional orders, Specky (back again; ambulance on its way) was swearing in a stream of unconsciousness. Seeing the couple's mate standing, looking numb, Dave yelled at the gathered gawkers, 'Get the f...ing bugger away from here!' The family who'd lost their butter and bacon led him off to their tent, Dave's voice ringing in their ears. 'Wrap him up and keep him calm. No alcohol.'

A man arrived dressed as if for a dinner party, and was about to get a volley but instead Dave just nodded towards the bloke Bill. The man took one look, gave a quiet 'Christ!' and set to work.

'How did you know he was a doctor?' Specky asked later on.

'Just did. And thank f... he came. You looked aboot ready tae spew yir ring.'

Not long after the doctor appeared there was a wailing of sirens and flashing lights dodged in and out between the tents. Ambulance. Police. From the Fort. Just down the glen – luckily.

'Imagine if it had happened up on Rannoch Moor!'

They were to do a great deal of imagining that night before they went to sleep.

After the ambulance had winked off into the near dark the police told everyone to get on with their lives and turned to Dave and Specky for their eye-witness account of what had happened. (A bewildered Hector, back from his hostel visit, listened.) The group stood between their tent and the charred wreckage, the pair beginning to shiver with both the growing chill of night and in nervous reaction. The more senior policeman shoved his notebook back in its pocket.

'Get yourselves warmed up a bit.'

Half an hour later he was done and repeated the action of shoving away his notebook, details noted, ready to go.

'Thanks for that report, lads; you did just fine. We're very grateful. And I'm sure those campers will be – one day.'

He actually held out a hand and they shook.

Wee Davy wasn't going to miss an opportunity, even if slightly taken aback at shaking hands 'wi the polis'. He said 'Och, we did precious little. Burns is affy. I'm a blacksmith. Ah ken,' then, in a butter-not-melting voice, 'Glad tae help ye. But I wonner if you'd be sae kind as tae run us doon tae the Fort. I'm thinkin a wee medicinal dram wouldna be oot o order.'

'We're not supposed to ... But what the hell? ... You'll all have to squeeze in the back.'

So they did. Seeing them go off with the police half the campsite jumped to wrong conclusions. By the time God's sun came up the resulting stories would not have been out place in Rupert Murdoch's *Sun*. When wee Dave went in to wash in the morning everyone else hurried out of the washroom. What might he not do next? That was really quite fortuitous for the amusement of *that*, for weeks after, largely balanced and then displaced the very real horror of the accident.

Expecting to sleep badly, of course they slept in – and missed the early morning train as a result. They sat for a couple of hours in Nevisport, they ambled up and down the High Street ('tempus not fugiting') and only relaxed properly when they went into the West Highland Museum and got thoroughly interested in a dozen topics. They went into a pub, which had better be nameless. When Dave came out from the loo he declared it was foul enough to be entered for the Turner Prize. They very nearly missed the midday train as well.

The Way Way walkers returning home were easily picked out. Once across Rannoch Moor they began going from side to side of the train shouting, 'Look! Look! Remember? Remember?' and from there to Tarbet they remained in that hyperactive state of grace. They took a great number of photographs, most of which would turn out to be reflections of themselves taking photographs ... Other passengers (mostly foreigners) looked at each other and shrugged, while others smiled, for they understood.

Notes

1. This was of course before the John Muir Trust stepped in to see that the summit remains in good heart.
2. The TGO Challenge is a coast-to-coast event in May. See Appendix 4.
3. BFs: members of the BFMC – Braes o' Fife Mountaineering Club.
4. This was prescience: Pitlochry Festival Theatre would stage the world première of *The Shellseekers* in 2001 – to Dave's critical approval.
5. This was the Forth and Clyde Junction Railway, Stirling to Balloch, opening in 1856 and closed to passengers in 1934.
6. John Napier (1550–1617) was the inventor of logarithms.
7. Robertson's *Tourist Guide* of 1858 noted that the island of Inchfad was 'for ladies whose peculiar relish for mountain dew precludes them from the unrestrained freedom of more populous districts'.
8. Duncryne, only 142 metres (460 feet), stands above Gartocharn, at the south end of Loch Lomond, a small hill with a huge, splendid view of the loch. Next time on the A811 take an hour off and climb the hill.
9. Naismith's Rule says to allow one hour for every three miles (5 km) of walking, plus half an hour for every 1000 feet (300 metres) of ascent.
10. 'Messages' are shopping/supplies in Lowland Scots.
11. The Gael's traditions and feelings of belonging, admiring, enjoying mountains were unknown to the rest of the world, which viewed them with some horror until the Romantic Movement changed attitudes.
12. Some details about Wade and Caulfeild are given in Appendix 2.
13. Easter 1892.
14. At present some trains do stop at Dalwhinnie.
15. The watershed, having run northwards up the east side of Loch Lomond (it bulges to round Loch Arklet and Cruach Ardrain) then sweeps over Beinn Laoigh before crossing the nameless pass above Tyndrum, follows the Bridge of Orchy Munros away east to round the Water of Tulla source,

then zooms west to Stob Ghabhar and Coire Ba before heading off across Rannoch Moor for Ben Alder.

16. Ladies Scottish Climbing Club. The book title mentioned is correct and her round trip was made in 1904 as she considered herself not up to stalking because of illness. She once shot six stags in a day, had one roll on top of her and bagged another on top of Ben Starav – and ran up enormous gambling debts. The book has recently been republished.

17. He could have had a point. In one West Highland estate between 1837 and 1840 the following were wiped out as 'vermin': 15 golden eagles, 27 white-tailed eagles, 18 ospreys, 98 sparrowhawks, 7 peregrine falcons, 11 hobbies, 275 kites, 5 marsh harriers, 63 goshawks, 285 common buzzards, 371 rough-legged buzzards, 3 honey buzzards, 462 kestrels, 78 merlins, 63 hen harriers, 6 gyrfalcons, 9 Montagu's harriers, 1,431 hooded crows, 475 ravens, 35 horned owls, 71 nightjars, 3 barn owls and 8 magpies.

18. What he saw was almost certainly the big tapering mast on the Binn above Burntisland. But a few years before when bombs went off *in Paris* American tourists stopped coming to *Scotland*.

19. The number is now reduced to ten.

20. The narrow ridge leading to Carn Mor Dearg has the designation Arête from traditional usage.

21. The CIC hut is the Charles Inglis Clark Memorial Hut, erected by the S.M.C. to commemorate a member killed in the First World War.

22. In a letter to his brother Tom, Keats wrote: 'Yesterday ... we went up Ben Nevis, the highest Mountain in Great Britain. On that account I will never ascend another ... 'twas the most vile descent – shook me all to pieces ...'.

23. The tin shelter has now been removed, and the summit is kept tidy by volunteers.

Appendix 1
The book list

This takes in all the books the party decided were the most important in any Scottish hillgoer's library, to which have been added some titles of particular relevance to the West Highland Way. The list is selective: natural history titles (birds, flowers, and so on) are largely omitted as a recent edition is advisable. The importance of many of these titles is seen in the fact that so many of them are still in print. This lists books up to the millennium only.

The party carried and used Robert Aitken's official guidebook. They quoted from it often enough, which is gratefully acknowledged. It has been reprinted several times since, edited by Robert Aitken and Roger Smith and includes a 1:25,000 Harvey map – still the best package for the Way Way.

Barrington, J., *Red Sky at Night* (1984). Shepherd's year described.
Bell, J. H. B., *A Progress in Mountaineering* (1950). Classic narrative/techniques.
Bennet, D., *The Munros* (SMC, 1999).
——, *The Southern Highlands* (SMC, 1991).
Borthwick, A., *Always a Little Further* (1939). Hilarious adventures.
Breadalbane, Marchioness of, *The High Tops of Black Mount* (1907). Victorian stalking days.
Brooker, W. D., *A Century of Scottish Mountaineering* (SMT 1988).
Brown, H. M., *Hamish's Mountain Walk* (1978, new edition 2010, Sandstone Press) and *Climbing the Corbetts* (1988, new edition 2012, Sandstone Press).
—— (ed.), *Poems of the Scottish Hills* (1982). Anthology.
—— and Berry, M., *Speak to the Hills* (1985). Anthology of 20th-century British/Irish poems.
Buchan, J., *The Massacre of Glencoe* (1933).

Burton, A., *The West Highland Way* (Aurum Press/OS, 1996). Guide.

Butterfield, I., *The Famous Highland Drove Walk* (1996).

——, *The Magic of the Munros* (1999). Large picture book.

Crocket, K., *Ben Nevis* (SMT, 1986). Comprehensive history.

Darling, F. and Boyd, M., *The Highlands and Islands* (New Naturalist Library, 1964). Good introduction to ecology.

Dempster, A., *The Grahams* (1997). Guide.

——, *The Munro Phenomenon* (1995).

Firsoff, V. A., *In the Hills of Breadalbane* (1954).

Gordon, Seton, *Highways and Byways in the West Highlands* (1935).

——, *Highways and Byways in the Central Highlands* (1949).

Haldane, A. R. B., *The Drove Roads of Scotland* (1952).

——, *New Ways Through the Glens* (1962). Both books: fascinating historical topics.

Harvey, C. and J., *Walks from the West Highland Railway* (1994).

Hewitt, D., *The Watershed Walk* (TACit Press, 1994).

HIDB: The Highlands and Islands Development Board (as was) produced several paperbacks as follows, well worth finding still. Nethersole-Thompson, D., *Highland Birds* (1974); Ratcliffe, D., *Highland Flora* (1977); Stephen, D., *Highland Animals* (1974); Price, R., *Highland Landforms* (1976).

Kilgour, W. T., *Twenty Years on Ben Nevis* (1905; Ernest Press, 1985). Observatory life.

Langmuir, E., *Mountaincraft and Leadership* (BMC). The best instructional manual, regularly updated.

Lindsay, M., *The Discovery of Scotland* (1964). Early travellers.

——, *The Eye is Delighted* (1971). Literary visitors.

——, *The Lowlands of Scotland: Glasgow and the North* (1979).

MacGill, P., *Children of the Dead End* (1914). Novel; Blackwater dam interest.

MacNally, L., *Highland Year*; *Highland Deer Forest*; *Wild Highlands*; *Year of the Red Deer*. Books which brought deer life to many.

Marsh, T., *The West Highland Way* (1999). Pocket-size guide.

Megarry, J., *The West Highland Way* (2000). Spiral bound; attractive.

Millman, R. N., *The Making of the Scottish Landscape* (1975).

Mitchell, I. R., *Scotland's Mountains Before the Mountaineers* (1998).

Mitchell, J., *Loch Lomondside* (New Naturalist Library, 2001).

Munro, Neil, *The New Road; John Splendid*. Classic novels touching Way areas.

Murray, W. H., *Rob Roy MacGregor: His Life and Times* (1982).

——, *Companion Guide to the West Highlands of Scotland* (1968, many reprints).

——, *Scotland's Mountains* (SMT, 1987). Interpretive.

——, *Mountaineering in Scotland* (1947) and *Undiscovered Scotland* (1951). Combined, Bâton Wicks publication, 1979.

Natural History of Loch Lomond (Glasgow University Press, 1974).

Nicolaisen, W. F. H., *Scottish Place Names* (1976).

Paterson, D. and McQueen, M., *The West Highland Way* (1992). Photographic account.

Prebble, J., *Glencoe: The Story of the Massacre* (1966).

——, *The Highland Clearances* (1963).

Scott, Walter, *Rob Roy*.

Smith, J. G., *The Parish of Strathblane ...* (1886).

——, *Strathendrick ...* (1896).

Steven, C. R., *The Story of Scotland's Hills* (1975).

Stevenson, R. L., *Kidnapped*. Great story touching the Way areas.

Stott, L., *The Waterfalls of Scotland* (1987).

Taylor, W., *The Military Roads in Scotland* (1996). Wade, Caulfeild, etc.

Thomas, J., *The Callander and Oban Railway* (1966).

——, *The West Highland Railway* (1965/1984).

Weir, T., *Highland Days* (1949). Early explorations.

——, *The Scottish Lochs* (1 volume, 1980).

Whittow, J., *Geology and Scenery in Scotland* (1992).

Wordsworth, Dorothy, *Recollections of a Tour Made in Scotland AD 1803* (1874).

Appendix 2

Wade and Caulfeild

Several times recently when people have been discussing the West Highland Way I've heard Wade's road over the Devil's Staircase mentioned. Perhaps West Highland Way walkers feel like echoing the lines attributed to Toby Caulfeild:

> If you'd seen these roads before they were made,
> You'd lift up your hands and bless General Wade.

However, the Devil's Staircase is *not* a Wade road, nor are several others which tend to be so credited. The following is an attempt to tidy up the facts about Wade and Caufeild, both of Irish families, who were successive road builders to the Scottish nation.

After the abortive risings of 1715 and 1719 various measures were taken to prevent a recurrence. In 1725 General Wade, Commander-in-Chief North Britain, who had already made a thorough survey of the Highlands, began the construction of roads and forts and barracks (like Ruthven) as part of his vision of controlling the clans.

He took just three summers to link Dunkeld and Inverness more or less on the line of our notorious A9. About two miles north of Dalnacardoch (Wade's headquarters for the A9 task), standing off the southbound lane, is Wade's Stone, a 7-foot commemorative monolith, dated 1729 (by layby 70).

His most famous landmark is the beautiful bridge he built at Aberfeldy, which was halfway along the Crieff–Dalnacardoch road he also built. Crieff was the great cattle tryst through those droving years but the Jacobite unrest saw the tryst moved to Falkirk.

In 1725 he raised the Black Watch at Aberfeldy, some 500 men of Clans Campbell, Grant, Fraser and Munro who were 'loyal' to the crown. They formed a sort of Highland constabulary: disarming the clans, preventing cattle reiving, guiding Sassenach forces and so on. They were drafted in to build his roads. He referred to them as his 'Highwaymen' and they received extra pay, and plenty of beer and beef, and there were some wild parties (with beasts roasted whole) when any stage was completed.

Before Wade went south to another post (and promotion to field marshal) he had constructed about 240 miles of road and twenty-eight bridges, quite a feat in just six years. Between the lines, I think Wade comes over as quite a decent bloke. He was still in the field in 1745 when that rebellion broke out and by an ironic twist of fate it was Prince Charlie's army that was the first to cross the Corrieyairack, Wade's most spectacular creation, linking Fort Augustus with the A9 route. Rising to nearly 2,000 feet, it was not the most practical road but it was used until Thomas Telford built the road we still use along by Loch Laggan and Roy Bridge.

The other major Wade road linked Fort William and Inverness, keeping east of the Great Glen lochs, and where this crossed the River Spean at High Bridge the first shots were fired in the 1745 rebellion. Wade was in England then. Sir John Cope's feeble efforts and ignominious defeat at Prestonpans led him to be court-martialled, Field Marshal Wade presiding.

Wade's bridge at Aberfeldy was designed by William Adam, the father of the famous architect sons, and it was intended as a showpiece. Most of Wade's bridges are simpler and functional rather than beautiful but some, like Garva Bridge on the Corrieyairack, are simple, functional *and* beautiful. Only Dorothy Wordsworth seems to have thought the Aberfeldy bridge ugly and she was aye girning.

At Weem across the valley from Aberfeldy, the hotel bears a picture of Wade, like an inn sign. He was based here at one time and many of his bases were made into stage houses, often 'King's Houses', which is why that name survives in several places today.

Caulfeild was Wade's able assistant and in 1732 he was made Inspector of Roads. He was on active service in the '45 and two years later became deputy to absentee Cumberland as governor of Inverness Castle. His work on roads continued until his death in 1767 – about 700 miles in all. His main routes were in two areas.

The longest began in Angus and went by Braemar and Cockbridge to Fort George with a continuation for Easter Ross through to Poolewe, so when you hear the radio saying the road from Cockbridge to Tomintoul is blocked, praise or blame Caulfeild! He also developed a whole system of roads from central Scotland into Argyll, including the one over Rannoch Moor and the Devil's Staircase to Fort William, and the Rest and Be Thankful road to Inveraray and Loch Fyne.

The military handed over to the civil in 1785 and the whole system was soon in disrepair. In 1803 Parliament set up a commission and appointed one Thomas Telford as engineer – but that is another story. There is a stone on top of the Rest and Be Thankful which commemorates the repairing of Caulfeild's original road. The line wends up below the present sweep of the A83.

Perhaps we can end with a quote, a stanza which is part of Britain's national anthem and was first sung in 1745 at the Drury Lane Theatre. (Ironically, the tune could have Jacobite origins!) The audience pleaded:

> God grant that Marshal Wade
> May by thy mighty aid
> Victory bring.
> May he sedition hush,
> And like a torrent rush,
> Rebellious Scots to crush,
> God save the King.

Appendix 3

The Rannoch Moor fiasco

The story of this crazy escapade was originally told in *Blackwood's Magazine* in 1927 and retold in two issues of the *Scottish Mountaineering Club Journal* in 1936 and 1937. The latter's resonant introduction explained it was the 'tale of a little band of seven determined men, with plenty of confidence in themselves, a lamentable contempt for the conditions, and a sublime disregard of the weather, who set out to cross the desolate Rannoch Moor and, as happens even to the unwisely bold, achieved their object'. The events took place at the end of January 1889.

There were three Forman & McCall engineers: Charles Forman (40), the surveyor James Bulloch (33) and a young assistant Harrison (28), Robert (later Sir Robert) McAlpine (41, the contractor and head of the famous firm), Major Martin of Kilmartin (40, factor of the Poltalloch Estates), John Bett (60, factor of the Breadalbane estates) and N. B. McKenzie (42), a Fort William solicitor, agent for the railway company.

They left Spean Bridge by coach and reached Inverlair Lodge mid-morning, then walked almost an hour to the end of Loch Treig. The landowner, Lord Abinger, had organised a boat to row them to the shooting lodge, at the south end of the loch, where they would spend the night. There was no sign of boat or boatman and when eventually he turned up (in time to stop them breaking down a boathouse door) their craft proved a tarred antique. Night and sleet fell on the party. Forman was unfit (he died of TB later) and all were clothed for town rather than country conditions. The younger gentlemen helped to row, others bailed the leaking water with their boots while cringing below umbrellas. Investigating a light, they grounded and two had to go into the water to free the craft. Eventually they were rescued by local keepers in their boat which took them to Craiguaineach Lodge. By then it was midnight.

Neither food nor beds were ready, the messenger, sent by the Lairig Leacach, not having arrived, and after eating as best they could, they passed the night under blankets while rain, hail and sleet blattered down, dawn bringing no improvement to the storm.

Unbelievably they continued: ferried over the first river as the bridge had been swept off, then facing a toilsome ascent to the edge of Rannoch Moor, beyond which lay twenty-three miles of 'weary-looking desert', as Robert Louis Stevenson called the Moor's mix of heather, bouldery hummocks, bogs and lochans. The lodge's keeper, having taken them up to the Moor, pointed into the wilds, and left them to it. Bulloch was the only one present who had any knowledge of the Moor. After four hours of squelching through the bogs and trudging the braes in the rain and sleet showers, they reached the River Gaur where, equally unbelievably, they had a planned noon business meeting with Sir Robert Menzies of Rannoch Lodge to discuss minor alignment problems of the route. Menzies, more sanely, sent his head keeper and invited them to Rannoch Lodge, at the west end of Loch Rannoch, for the night. Ahead, there still lay fourteen miles to Inveroran with only one cottage eight miles off between, and three hours of daylight remaining. They decided to carry on!

They were ferried over the River Gaur near its outflow from Loch Laidon at 1.30 p.m. The Gaur is the main eastward drainage of the Moor, well-described as the 'birthplace of many waters'. The weather remained wild and wet. They straggled on, each choosing his own line.

Towards dusk they realised their mistake. They were floundering, unable to pick out details, falling full length at times, becoming tired, soaked, cold and depressed, Bett and McKenzie being helped by the fitter members of the party. Eventually Bett could go no further. The major and Harrison stayed with him, their shelter the old man's umbrella; Forman and McKenzie struggled on but soon sought shelter in the lee of a boulder; while McAlpine and Bulloch took separate ways onwards, the former aiming for Inveroran, the latter hoping to strike Gorton where he knew of a cottage from a previous survey.

Bulloch, several hours later, collapsed over a fence and lay stunned for four hours then, recovering, groped his way along the fence, found a track – and reached Gorton. Out on the Moor Bett had fallen unconscious and the other two only kept warm by running in circles. At one stage they lost sight of Bett so marked his position by tying a white handkerchief to his brolly, before continuing their athletic circlings.

About 2.30 a.m. they noticed lights and lit matches, which were spotted by the two Gorton shepherds dispatched by Bulloch. They and their dog then found Forman and McKenzie and, half carrying, half dragging Bett, they headed for a wooden hut two miles off, on the Avon Dubh. There was an old stove and some peats inside and they managed to light a fire, only to be nearly asphyxiated, till one of the shepherds removed a peat which had been placed over the top of the chimney. The stove became red hot. The shepherds then returned to Gorton and were back at daybreak with food and drinks. By 10.30 a.m. the railway party were recovered enough to set out again and reached Gorton at noon. Their anxiety about McAlpine was eased and the search party stood down when a messenger brought word that he was safe in a cottage three miles down the Tulla. He'd arrived soaked to the skin and covered in mud after fourteen hours floundering alone on the Moor.

Using a cart for Bett, they moved on, collecting McAlpine *en passant*, and eventually reached Inveroran nine miles to the west. The snow was already falling and that night a blizzard raged; had it come the night before there would have been a certain tragedy. Next day they had to struggle through huge drifts to make Tyndrum for the Callander and Oban train.

Their line was built, however, and opened in 1894. Across the Moor much of it had to be 'floated' on brushwood as no bottom could be found in the peat. Storms often overwhelmed traffic between Loch Treig and Gorton in the years ahead. Gorton had an old passenger coach used as a school, with eleven children attending at one stage. Serious proposals were also made for running a railway line up to the summit of Ben Nevis. After all, the Forth Bridge had been opened in 1890. One can only wonder at the self-confidence of the Victorians. The story is also told in John Thomas: *The West Highland Railway.*

Appendix 4

The TGO Challenge

This is an annual Backpacking Event which encourages people to design and then go and walk a route, coast-to-coast across Scotland, starting anywhere between Ardrishaig and Torridon and finishing anywhere between Arbroath and Fraserburgh. The event has taken place each May since 1979 and entry is via a form in the October issue of *TGO* (*The Great Outdoors* magazine, the event sponsor), which will also carry highlights, in words and pictures, of that year's event. Numbers are limited, with a percentage of 'old hands' always included. Route and style are up to the individual walker or group (maximum four). Since it is held in May, lambing means dogs are not allowed. Routes planned are submitted for 'vetting' by experts who can offer advice and participants check in at a dozen starting points on the West Coast and, after finishing on the East Coast, check in at Montrose (usually in celebratory fashion!). The lower age for entry is eighteen and there is no upper age limit. One ninety-year-old has made a crossing, several crossings have been made by blind walkers and over thirty people have made ten or more crossings. The friendly event was set up to encourage people to make longer treks, with their great rewards, and as a direct contribution to the social and economic life in the Highlands. More energetic walkers have the option of a High Level route, which will take in ten Munros and/or Corbetts, and everyone, whatever route chosen, must finish within the two-week span. However tackled, the event *is* always a Challenge (a marvellously friendly one), the perfect lure for those wanting to 'do their own thing', and a natural progression from set routes like the West Highland Way.

More books for walkers and lovers of the outdoors...

'...this is no stuffy tome. The book is a delight. Much more than a mere travelogue, the journey is the thread along which the narrative is woven. Hamish's affection for the Berber people and their country is apparent and he shares with the reader anecdotes and knowledge accumulated over the years. ...It's an essential aid for planning expeditions, supplies background information for anyone joining an organised trek, and is a good read for armchair travellers'. *John Muir Trust Journal*

'It was an epic undertaking by a man with a powerful personal attachment to that part of the world. However, *The Mountains Look on Marrakech* is not the story of a lone traveller in a dry and dusty wilderness - far from it. It is rooted in a sense of camaraderie and shared experience while celebrating a richly varied environment, the descriptions of which will amaze anyone who believes Morocco is (to use Brown's words) "all camels and kasbahs". ...vivid and compelling record ...an engaging storyteller ... Supplemented by maps and colour photographs, *The Mountains Look on Marrakech* is a delightful volume which clearly falls into the "labour of love" category'. *Caithness Courier and The Northern Times*

978-184995-084-8   240 × 170mm   304 pages   16pp colour section   softback £19.99

To order go to www.whittlespublishing.com, e-mail info@whittlespublishing.com or telephone 01593-731333

'*Seton Gordon's Cairngorms* is culled from a lifetime of his writing about the special range, and is illustrated with archival photographs that complement the selected prose. ... Everyone with a love of the outdoors will find this book a joy. Hamish Brown has used his own considerable experience to create a memorable companion volume to *Seton Gordon's Scotland* (also published by Whittles Publishing).'
St. Andrews in Focus

978-1904445-88-3   *240 × 170mm   226 pages liberally illustrated, inc. some original b/w photos   hardback   £25.00*

'...it is a kaleidoscope of a way of life in the first half of the 20th century, a contribution of great importance. There are customs, myths, fairy stories and legends to fascinate anyone in the HIghlands and Islands and beyond. ...An utterly fascinating book'.
Highland News

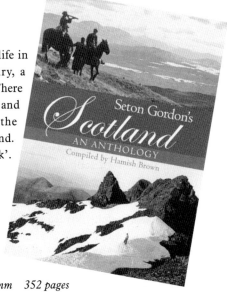

978-1904445-73-9   *240 × 170mm   352 pages liberally illustrated using original photographs softback   £19.99*

978-184995-031-2   234 × 156mm   208 pages
illustrated with photographs and maps
softback   £16.99

'...The appeal in the book for me was the other walks which make up the bulk of the content. These give alternatives to Munros and Corbetts: ideal for half days and taking visitors perhaps not used to hillwalking. ... this book is ideal'. ***Munro Society Newsletter***

'...The book is ideal for suggesting options that are a bit further afield ... in the main the routes described are not more than 5 hours ... refreshment spots are suggested...' ***Kirkintilloch Mountaineering Club***

'...The narrative which accompanies each of the walks makes for entertaining reading. ...Usefully divided into different areas, with full page maps at the start of each section, this is a book to inspire walkers and to delight the armchair traveller too'. ***Scottish Home & Country***